B2B
EXCHANGES

Earlier

B2B EXCHANGES

The Killer Application in the Business-to-Business Internet Revolution

ARTHUR B. SCULLEY *and*
W. WILLIAM A. WOODS

HarperBusiness
An Imprint of HarperCollins*Publishers*

B2B EXCHANGES. Copyright © 2001 by Arthur B. Sculley and W. William A. Woods. All rights reserved. Printed in the United States of America. No part of this book may be used or reproduced in any manner whatsoever without written permission except in the case of brief quotations embodied in critical articles and review. For information, address HarperCollins Publishers, Inc., 10 East 53rd Street, New York, NY 10022.

HarperCollins books may be purchased for educational, business, or sales promotional use. For information please write: Special Markets Department, HarperCollins Publishers, Inc., 10 East 53rd Street, New York, NY 10022.

FIRST EDITION

Designed by Stratford Publishing Services

Library of Congress Cataloging-in-Publication Data

Sculley, Arthur B.
    B2B exchanges : the killer application in the business-to-busi   on /
Arthur B. Sculley and W. William A. Woods.
    p.   cm.
    Originally published: Hamilton, Bermuda : ISI Publications, 199
    Includes bibliographical references and index.
    ISBN 0-06-662108-9
    1. Industrial marketing.   2. Business enterprises—Computer networks.   3. Internet marketing.   I. Title: B to B exchanges.   II. Title: Killer application in the business-to-business internet revolution.   III. Woods, William A.   IV. Title.

HF5415.1263 .S38 2001
658.8'4—dc21   00-054021

01 02 03 04 05   10 9 8 7 6 5 4 3 2 1

Contents

Part I
DEFINING THE B2B MARKET SPACE

Part II
ANATOMY OF A B2B EXCHANGE

Part III
SEVEN SECRETS FOR SUCCESS
FOR B2B EXCHANGES

Part IV
THE FUTURE OF B2B

Acknowledgments

For their role in the preparation of this book we wish especially to thank Dave Conti, our editor at HarperBusiness, and his superb team. Our heartfelt thanks also to Sarah Barham, Ian Hallsworth, and Carol Bonnet at ISI Publications for having faith in our ideas and working tirelessly to ensure that the hardback edition became a best-seller. However, we take responsibility for any errors or omissions that remain.

Foreword

After his retirement from JP Morgan, my brother, Arthur, agreed to become the nonexecutive chairman of the Bermuda Stock Exchange, which is where he and William Woods—with his extensive stock exchange experience—first started to work together on what has become a successful undertaking: to transform a sleepy, local island stock exchange into a global stock exchange powered by the Internet.

I wish I could say that I fully appreciated five years ago how important Internet business-to-business (B2B) exchanges would become. Today it is obvious that B2B, and especially Internet, exchanges, wherein commodities, financial instruments, intellectual properties, and various other goods and services are electronically traded, are one of the most important pillars of the new economy.

What most distinguishes the new economy from the old one is the shift in power from producers to customers, who now are in control of everything. Customers can demand—and expect to receive—the best quality, best service, and lowest prices; they also want everything customized, and they want it immediately. The Internet enables commerce to work on a truly global scale. Entrepreneurs can fundamentally reinvent how work gets done and give customers whatever they demand. The competition is no longer between big and small but between fast and slow. Innovation is rewarded, while traditional business size and stature are more often baggage than an advantage.

This revolution may be likened to the invention of movable type more than five hundred years ago, but with one big difference: This change is much larger and is happening much faster than anything the world has ever experienced. Business-to-consumer (B2C) companies certainly grabbed the world's attention during the 1990s, but many highly credible industry analysts forecast that the impact of B2B Internet companies will be many times larger than that of B2C.

The first wave of web companies was based on unique enabling technologies, such as browsers, search engines, auctions, e-mail, chat, and various portal services. Building recognizable Internet brands set the pace, so it's not surprising that these first-generation Internet companies were started by high-tech entrepreneurs and backed by respected high-tech venture capitalists. But as the Internet moves toward B2B, it is now clear that traditional, large companies have no choice but to get into the game. In the first decade of the twenty-first century, we will see most corporations rush to reinvent themselves. We will see global service economy centers like New York, Chicago, London, and Frankfurt jockey for position to lead various sectors of the Internet B2B industries. Small nations and regions, such as Hong Kong, Singapore, Israel, Ireland, Taiwan, Scandinavia, Australia, New Zealand, and Bermuda, with their advantage of speed, are also racing to become players in the new economy. We will see B2B exchanges becoming an important building block in the B2B global economy.

The best new companies will be those that take advantage of the Internet's unique strengths. Real-time, interactive communications and transactions that can be executed one-to-one are good examples. The Internet's power lies also in its ability to track and build histories as well as dynamically form cooperative buying groups, transact auctions, and provide instant up-to-date information for informed deal making.

I have learned a lot from my brother's experience in B2B exchanges, which we at Sculley Brothers LLC are now trying to adopt and apply in derivative forms to some of our other Internet companies, both B2B and B2C. Anyone who intends to build companies in the new economy will find this book to be an extraordinarily useful and insightful guide.

John Sculley
Partner
Sculley Brothers LLC

Introduction

In the last five years we have studied and set up many business-to-business "exchanges," "e-markets," or "net markets" on the Internet. We have chosen to call these new on-line markets "B2B exchanges." As B2B exchanges moved from obscurity to the front pages of the *Wall Street Journal* and "new economy" magazines such as *Business 2.0,* we realized that between us we have several areas of expertise that when combined create a potentially powerful knowledge set for any entrepreneur or company that wants to establish or develop a B2B exchange.

Our securities market experiences, working with a number of stock exchanges over the last 16 years, are particularly relevant. Just as tremors warn of an impending earthquake, the upheaval in the securities markets that Internet-based, electronic trading systems are causing is a signal of the huge changes that are now beginning to appear in every major industry. The fact that electronic systems are shaking the very foundations of centuries-old stock exchange institutions should be a warning that no industry or company, however established it may be, will be spared. Every business will be shaken by this Internet quake.

The more we analyzed these new B2B exchanges, the more we realized that they are the "killer application" of the B2B Internet revolution. This is clearly demonstrated in the moves by established bricks and mortar businesses to set up B2B exchanges (either on their own or in industry consortia) as part of their growing acceptance of the Internet, Internet standards, and the new economy generally.

These new Internet-based exchanges can learn a lot from the way that stock exchanges have been structured and operated in the last three hundred years. And there are a lot of things that B2B exchanges must learn *not* to do from securities markets—especially in light of the economic dynamics of increasing returns that are shaping the new economy.

In this book we set out the core principles of success for these new exchanges so they can seize this unique opportunity and develop rapidly. In a "winner takes most" economy it is critical to move quickly, and we hope that by adopting the Seven Secrets of Success we present in this book, the entrepreneurs and industry consortia that are starting B2B exchanges can achieve success. It has given us enormous satisfaction that many readers of the hardback edition of this book considered it the bible for their business plans. We had no idea when we wrote the book that it would become a best-seller, and we would like to thank everyone who bought it.

Since the hardback was published, debate has arisen over two issues. The first is the emergence of industry consortia exchanges—and whether they are able to operate as neutral markets. The second is the increasing regulatory attention that B2B exchanges are attracting.

Industry consortia have the major advantage that they are well funded by their bricks and mortar parents. Nevertheless, these attempts to start B2B exchanges face the same challenges that the entrepreneurial ones do. We analyze these challenges from the point of view of industry consortia in a completely new Chapter 16.

Regulatory challenges include Federal Trade Commission and European Union review of B2B exchanges from the antitrust perspective. In a new Chapter 17 we analyze the antitrust issues raised by successful B2B exchanges.

In this book we draw mainly on examples from the United States, because that is where the new economy is developing the fastest. However, the business transformation that we describe is occurring worldwide and has started to accelerate in Europe and Asia as companies learn from U.S. experience and fight to catch up.

This book is meant for senior management in Industrial Age companies that are setting up B2B exchanges as industry consortia and for entrepreneurs who want to build their own B2B exchange, as well as for potential investors in B2B exchanges. We hope that this paperback version will also appeal to the wider public and in some way help people shape their own destiny and that of their employers.

B2B exchanges are emerging and evolving in Internet time. That is, some of what we say is going out of date even as you read it. For this reason we have launched a web site, www.b2bexchanges.com, to complement and update the information in this book as frequently as possible. We hope that our web site will become a central information source for everyone involved in this exciting area, and particularly that it will be an important on-line networking opportunity for B2B exchanges.

Part I

DEFINING THE B2B MARKET SPACE

CHAPTER 1

What Are B2B Exchanges?

Corporations' acceptance of the Internet in the new economy has sparked a revolution in the way businesses buy and sell products from each other. These business-to-business, or B2B, transactions are increasingly being done over Internet-based net markets, or B2B exchanges. If today's bricks and mortar companies are to survive, they must reinvent themselves to integrate the Internet into everything they do and connect with one or more B2B exchanges.

THE JARGON JUNGLE

The Internet Revolution, or new economy, has created many new companies, produced thousands of new millionaires, and captured investors' attention to the point where it seems that every New York taxi driver is a day trader with some on-line brokerage service. Initially, investors' attention was focused on companies that sell goods or services to the general public—what are now commonly called "business-to-consumer," or B2C, transactions—or enable consumers to sell goods or services to each other—a "consumer-to-consumer," or C2C, model. Another new economic model is a "consumer-to-business," or C2B, model, in which the consumer states the price.

B2B: Business to business, as in B2B exchanges
B2C: Business to consumer, as in Amazon.com
C2C: Consumer to consumer, as in users of eBay.com
C2B: Consumer to business, as in Priceline.com

Good examples of B2C companies are Amazon.com, Inc. (www.amazon.com), the on-line bookstore, and America Online, Inc. (www.aol.com), the Internet service and on-line content provider. A well-known example of a C2C company is eBay, Inc. (www.ebay.com), the popular on-line auctions company. eBay offers one big, virtual consumer trading community where individuals can buy and sell things from one another in auctions. An example of a C2B company is Priceline (www.priceline.com), where consumers indicate the price at which they are willing to buy a variety of goods and services, including airline tickets.

In this book we demystify the jargon and discuss the nature of business-to-business solutions on the Internet, that is, B2B transactions. Some people, especially outside the United States, still regard the Internet as some sort of academic experiment or, at best, a low-security replacement for the telephone that allows individuals to send e-mails to each other. But in the last four years, especially in the United States, the reliability and security issues associated with the early use of the Internet have been largely solved and every business is now adopting the Internet in one form or another. Now some innovative new uses of the Internet by business are revolutionizing the way in which many goods and services are procured, priced, and distributed.

The quiet revolution that is developing in the world of B2B transactions will generate far more profits and millionaires than anything the C2C, B2C, and C2B models can produce and will have a far more profound impact on the economy of each country than any number of Amazon.coms.

THE POWER OF THE NETWORK

Powering this alphabet soup is a collection of silicon chips, copper wire, and glass fiber that is generically called a "network." The network links all Internet-connected computers (more than 200 million worldwide), as well as an increasing range of everyday devices, such as mobile phones and fridges, that have silicon chips built into them (presently more than two billion worldwide). The network currently operates in accordance with the suite of communications standards called the Transmission Control Protocol/Internet Protocol, or TCP/IP.

Bob Metcalfe, the inventor of another networking standard called Ethernet, was the first person to notice that the value of a network increases by the square of the number of people or things connected to it.

In other words, as the number of connections on a network increases linearly, the value of that network to its members increases on a compounding, or exponential, basis. If you owned a fax machine at a time when only two such machines existed, its value to you was modest. If you own a fax machine today, when there are more than 200 million of them connected to the phone network, the ability to send and receive from each of those 200 million machines—a total of $(200m - 1)^2$ possible connections—makes your machine exponentially more valuable to you. Incidentally, the Internet is so fundamentally changing the way companies communicate with each other that you may soon decide to consign your fax machine to the same storage cupboard where that old telex machine sits.

Kevin Kelly, in his insightful book *New Rules for the New Economy,* points out that the value of a network like the Internet actually increases faster than Metcalfe's formula of n^2, where n is the number of people connected. Metcalfe's network law is based on a telephone or fax network, where connections are point to point between two people. On an electronic network, we can make multiple simultaneous connections between groups of people (including ourselves) so that the potential value of the network is not just $n \times n$, but n^n. We call this "Kelly's new law of networks."

The most dynamic example of this type of network is an online exchange, where multiple buyers and multiple sellers come together in a virtual trading space. The potential value of a neutral B2B exchange is thus n^n, where n is the number of users connected to that exchange.

THE INTERNET CHANGES EVERYTHING

Once a company starts to integrate the Internet into what it does, everything changes for the company. Change starts with the way in which employees communicate with one another. Next to change is the way the company sells and distributes its products, and then the way the company communicates with other companies, for example, the way it communicates with its suppliers, the way it procures the goods and services it needs, and the way in which it manages its whole supply chain management process, including inventory control and logistics. Finally, the Internet enables companies to move away from fixed pricing to dynamic pricing models, for example, through the use of B2B exchanges. This allows buying companies to significantly lower their acquisition costs, reduce inventory levels, and ensure more on-time delivery of their products.

Buying companies are becoming far more demanding as the Internet creates a historic shift of power from the seller to the buyer.

B2B MARKETS ARE ENORMOUS

The potential for B2B e-commerce is already much larger than that for B2C transactions, and it is predicted to grow much more rapidly.

Many B2B markets are enormous. For example, each year in the United States the market for paper is worth at least $260 billion, the market for steel is at least $600 billion, and the market for plastics is $370 billion. In contrast, the U.S. market for books is worth just $25 billion per year.

In the first edition of this book, we predicted that the total of on-line transactions facilitated by B2B exchanges will exceed $600 billion in value (40% of an estimated on-line total of $1.5 trillion) by 2004 in the United States alone: If B2B exchanges capture revenues representing just 0.5% of this turnover, they will collectively generate $3 billion in revenue per annum by 2004—and that excludes the rest of the world!

By way of comparison, Forrester Research has estimated that total B2C on-line commerce in the United States will reach just $108 billion by 2003.

B2B EXCHANGES

The power of the Network has resulted in the emergence of centralized marketplaces where businesses can buy and sell goods and services from each other. Following the logic of calling centralized markets for the trading of stocks and bonds stock exchanges, we have named these exciting new business-to-business markets *B2B exchanges*. Within the overall B2B revolution the unique features of these on-line exchanges are not yet fully appreciated. In this book we analyze the profound changes that are occurring in B2B transactions as a result of the development of these Internet-based B2B exchanges.

Because they're able to bring buyers and sellers together on-line from all over the world and thereby to create dynamic pricing, cost reductions, and process improvements, B2B exchanges are the killer application in the B2B Internet revolution.

DEFINING A B2B EXCHANGE

The *New Shorter Oxford English Dictionary* defines *exchange* as "a building, office, institution, etc., used for the transaction of business or for monetary exchange."

On the Internet, every web site that enables buyers and sellers to come together and find each other is a virtual exchange building. In this book we explain the phenomenon of formal B2B exchanges as they are developing on the web and describe the anatomy of a model B2B exchange. We then analyze the key issues in building a credible and successful B2B exchange.

What, exactly, is a B2B exchange? Unlike the proverbial elephant, you may not know one when you see one! We will now set out a clear definition of a B2B exchange and distinguish such an exchange from the tens of thousands of standard B2B e-commerce companies that already exist.

The unique feature of a B2B exchange is that it brings many buyers and sellers together in one central virtual market space

and enables them to buy and sell from each other at a dynamic price that is determined in accordance with the rules of the exchange.

The main thing that differentiates a B2B exchange from other B2B e-commerce companies is that an exchange involves *multiple* buyers and sellers in a many-to-many model—it centralizes and matches buy and sell orders and provides posttrade information. Contrast this with the procurement process of one company, say, General Motors, which sets up a web site with an auction process for suppliers to bid on contracts with GM. Although this is a B2B e-commerce site, it is NOT a B2B exchange, because there is only one buyer. Similarly, because there is only one seller, a business that offers goods or services for sale to other businesses over the Internet is not an exchange, even if it provides a price-setting mechanism that is normally associated with an exchange, such as an auction.

Together GM, Ford, Nissan, Renault, and DaimlerChrysler are in the process of setting up an on-line exchange called Covisint, where they and other automotive manufacturers can buy parts from multiple suppliers—that will be a true B2B exchange as we have defined it.

Having multiple buyers and sellers creates its own special effects and necessitates a specialized approach to building a successful B2B exchange versus a successful B2B e-commerce company. For example, as we explore in Chapters 5 and 11, an exchange must remain neutral and balance the competing interests of all its users—buyers, sellers, shareholders, and brokers—and sometimes also take into consideration the public good.

Although we call these new, virtual marketplaces "exchanges," they generally do not fall within the definition of a stock exchange or commodities exchange and are not subject to registration with and regulation by government regulators, such as the U.S. Securities and Exchange Commission (SEC), that supervise securities markets and stock exchanges. B2B exchanges are facilitating trades in goods and services such as paper, chemicals, and insurance.

Four years ago, there were no B2B exchanges outside of the securities markets. Today there are more than one thousand such exchanges operating on the Internet.

Prominent B2B exchanges that we refer to throughout this book are BigMachines, Catex, CreditTrade, e-STEEL, FreeMarkets, Metal-Site, PaperExchange, PlasticsNet, and TechEx. We have been involved as founders of, investors in, advisors to, or business partners in some of these exchanges. This book presents our current knowledge and experience of B2B exchanges and our experience in developing the Bermuda Stock Exchange as a fully electronic exchange for the trading of securities.

THE WINNER TAKES MOST

Dr. James Martin, the author of *Cybercorp: The New Business Revolution,* has published a new book, *After the Internet: Alien Intelligence,* in which he demonstrates that the largest player, or "winner," in a particular vertical space will come to dominate that vertical because success is self-reinforcing in the new economy. This powerful new paradigm derives from the fact that on a computer network, success is driven by the dynamics of increasing returns rather than by the old laws of diminishing returns that plague Industrial Age companies.

As with securities markets, the more competing buyers and sellers that can be brought together in one place, the more liquid a market becomes and the more efficient the price-setting mechanism is. This creates a self-reinforcing mechanism whereby the sellers are attracted to the market with the most potential buyers and the increase in sellers makes that market space more attractive to more buyers, and so on—resulting in more transactions in that market.

Liquidity is king in the land of B2B exchanges and, in accordance with the law of increasing returns, the most liquid exchange will be the winner.

The ubiquity and ease of use of the Internet mean that people no longer have to be brought onto one physical trading floor to create liquidity. Increasingly inexpensive computing power and telecommunications are the weapons that allow Internet-based trading networks to challenge traditional trading mechanisms.

B2B exchanges create an electronic, virtual marketplace that we call a "market space." Increasing returns will lead to a concentration of buyers and sellers in one B2B exchange market space for each product.

One B2B exchange may operate several market spaces, but only one market space is likely to dominate for each product.

ARE ELECTRONIC COMMUNICATIONS NETWORKS B2B EXCHANGES?

One form of electronic trading that has attracted a lot of publicity in the traditional media to date is the electronic communications network, or ECN. ECNs are alternative securities trading systems that are generally privately owned and offer fully automated order routing and trade execution services. In effect, they are mini stock exchanges, but they don't like to call themselves that and don't offer all the services of a traditional stock exchange, because the SEC has not registered them as such in the United States. ECNs such as Archipelago Holdings, Instinet, and Island offer a central market space where buy and sell orders are automatically matched; any order that does not match in the ECN is automatically routed onto another ECN or to a traditional stock exchange for execution. In our analysis, ECNs are definitely a form of exchange, but they are not solely

B2B exchanges. In the United States, ECNs provide many institutional investors with anonymous trading opportunities, but they are also aimed at providing retail investors with low-cost execution-only services, in addition to extended trading hours and links to multiple exchanges. Therefore, according to our definitions, ECNs are a hybrid between a B2C exchange and a B2B exchange.

ECNs have grown rapidly: There are now more than 50 alternative trading systems in the United States, of which 9 are registered as ECNs—Archipelago, Instinet, Island, and Strike, to name just a few leading systems. Recent SEC reports indicate that ECNs now trade more than 25% of Nasdaq's volume and 5% of the NYSE's.

ECNs have captured a greater share of Nasdaq's volume because they offer a more efficient price discovery function than do the market-makers on Nasdaq. ECNs directly match buyers and sellers at the price that each is offering rather than at the bid–offer spread of the Nasdaq market-maker (who keeps the difference in the spread). The NYSE uses specialists to match buyers' and sellers' orders, but, because it has greater liquidity, only about 10% of trades are made with the specialist. The remaining 90% of trades are matched directly at the buyer's and seller's offered price, which means that it is more efficient at setting the market price and, so far, has lost less market share to ECNs.

In this book we use several lessons suggested by the success of ECNs to illustrate the Seven Secrets of Success for other B2B exchanges, but we do not analyze specific ECNs in depth; they are a special phenomenon of securities markets and warrant their own dedicated study. However, given that stock exchanges are one of the oldest forms of formal exchange market, the rapid success of ECNs and their dynamic effects on more traditional stock exchanges are extremely important indicators of the potential for B2B exchanges.

MORE EFFICIENT PRICE DISCOVERY

In the industrial economy, most prices are fixed by the seller, who publishes a catalog with nonnegotiable prices. An alternative method to determine the price is to bring all the potential buy and sell orders together and let their competing offers set the highest price or the price that maximizes the amount sold. This is the approach adopted by ECNs with their central market-matching systems for securities. It is also the price discovery mechanism adopted by eBay to run its on-line auctions for consumers.

Increasingly, dynamic price-setting mechanisms are being used by many B2B exchanges for B2B transactions, because the Internet's ability to interconnect companies cheaply means that an Internet exchange can bring together bids and offers from all over the world.

In the new economy, there has been a significant shift in economic power from the seller to the buyer. This is as true for B2B transactions as it is for B2C, C2C, and C2B. On the Internet this truism is evident in the rapid rise of "reverse," or buyer-driven, auctions. As we explore in Chapter 6, these auctions enable the buyer—for example, a company seeking to procure supplies—to solicit bids from multiple suppliers and watch the competition between those suppliers driving the procurement price downward as the close of the auction approaches (hence the name "reverse auction"). B2B exchanges are adopting reverse auctions to attract key buyers with the lure of substantial cost reductions for those big players.

REGULATING THE MARKET

Providing an open and fair market with complete transparency is a key element of an exchange's value proposition and enhances the exchange's ability to attract business. The exchange can ensure that it is open and fair only if it is prepared to regulate the users of it's centralized market facility. The form of regulation most appropriate for Internet-based exchanges is what we call "self-regulation," whereby the B2B exchange should be a self-regulatory organization, or SRO.

In Chapter 12, we explain that a successful B2B exchange must regulate its own members in order to build credibility and integrity and avoid calls for outside regulation.

When a B2B exchange brings together several large bricks and mortar companies in the same industry, particularly as large shareholders, there may be the potential for antitrust abuses. This is now a key issue for regulators such as the Federal Trade Commission in the United States and the European Union.

WHY B2B WILL ALWAYS BE LESS VISIBLE THAN B2C

Amazon.com, eBay, and Yahoo! are already household names around the world. Companies like BigMachines, Catex, CreditTrade, e-STEEL, MetalSite, PaperExchange, and TechEx are unknown to the general public, but are relatively well known in their industries. Why is this? One obvious reason is that B2C companies market and sell to consumers, so we all hear about what they do. B2B exchanges deal only with other businesses in their specific vertical industry sector, so they are naturally less visible to consumers and the media.

In 2000, this began to change. An increasing number of media articles referred to the B2B revolution, and an increasing number of securities analysts focused on B2B e-commerce. Wall Street decided that B2C companies would not make profits for a long time to come while B2B companies could be profitable more quickly. For those investors, particularly institutional investors, who missed out on the B2C dotcom phenomenon, B2B investing became the opportunity to make sure they were not going to be left out this time.

When we started writing this book, B2B was a hot subject that was becoming a red hot subject. In 2000, B2B captured the imagination of Wall Street. Suddenly, B2B companies were a sexy investment trend. Commerce One and Ariba, two leading providers of infrastructure and systems to B2B exchanges, went public in highly successful IPOs. Commerce One attained a market value in excess of $15 billion on 1999 revenues of just $33 million. In February 2000, Chemdex, a former high-profile B2B exchange in the chemicals sector, changed its name to Ventro and announced that it would be launching new B2B exchanges in related verticals. As a result, the share price went up 100% to $240 and the company released another announcement to emphasize that there had been no actual financial transactions involved in the name change. This was the high point of Wall Street's sudden but brief love affair with B2B.

Like all investment fads, the B2B fever passed, and the B2B sector is no longer the darling of the Wall Street analysts. Share prices of the B2B stocks fell heavily after April 2000: For example, Commerce One's share price fell to about 75% of its 52-week high, and Ventro shares fell more than 99% to below $2 in December 2000.

However, the B2B Internet revolution had begun long before Wall Street learned about it, and the revolution is continuing now unabated by Wall Street's loss of favor. The dramatic impact that B2B exchanges and B2B companies will have in every industry is only just beginning to emerge, and the key messages of this book remain valid.

If you're following the Internet commerce revolution, take it from us—you ain't seen nothin yet!

CHAPTER SUMMARY

- B2B means business-to-business. B2C = Amazon.com, C2C = eBay.com, and C2B = Priceline.com.
- B2B e-commerce means potentially larger profits and cost savings than B2C markets.
- Bob Metcalfe's law of networks identified compounding growth in networks. Kevin Kelly's "new law of networks" identifies the additional exponential growth in the value of Internet networks.
- The Internet changes everything for companies.
- B2B markets are enormous compared to B2C transactions, and B2B on-line transactions will grow at a much faster pace than B2C transactions.
- We previously predicted that the value of B2B transactions passing through B2B exchanges will exceed $600 billion by 2004 in the United States alone. If B2B exchanges capture revenues representing just 0.5% of this turnover, they will collectively generate $3 billion in revenue per annum by 2004—and that excludes the rest of the world.
- Thanks to the ubiquitous Internet technology, a large number of new companies are now establishing themselves as formal B2B exchanges on the web.
- What is a B2B exchanges? The unique feature of a B2B exchange is that it brings multiple buyers and sellers together in a central virtual market space and enables them to buy and sell from each other at a dynamic price that is determined in accordance with the rules of the exchange.
- Electronic communications networks, or ECNs, are exchanges but not strictly B2B exchanges.
- B2B exchanges must be differentiated from B2B e-commerce companies that offer products for sale or seek to procure

products on-line but represent only one buyer or one seller so that they do not bring multiple buyers and sellers together.

- Increasing returns mean that the winner will take most in each vertical space.
- The media hype about B2B may have subsided, but the B2B Internet revolution continues unabated.

CHAPTER 2

On-line, B2B Is Where the Profits Will Be

In Chapter 1 we identified the acronyms that have been created to describe certain features of the new economy. In this chapter, we establish the size of the B2B market space and describe how the Internet is revolutionizing B2B transactions.

Businesses are increasingly adopting Internet solutions for many reasons:

- Interactive networks are now ubiquitous and inexpensive.
- Companies are becoming increasingly familiar with Internet technologies.
- There are low barriers of entry for companies to adopt Internet-based strategies.

In this chapter we explore how on-line B2B transactions in general are revolutionizing work flow patterns and will generate cost savings and increased profits on the Internet. We estimate the size of the B2B market space and describe the changes the Internet is bringing about in corporations. If you know about B2B generally and want to get right into the details of B2B exchanges, skip this chapter and go straight to Chapter 3.

- Industry-wide standards such as Extensible Markup Language (XML) are emerging that are cheaper, faster, and better than the old Electronic Data Interchange (EDI) standards.
- The Internet is the ultimate global distribution system.
- Companies are hearing about or actually experiencing incredible cost savings and new revenue opportunities on-line.
- The Internet offers companies the opportunity to revolutionize their supply chain management.

As more companies adopt Internet-based B2B applications, other companies will have to follow them just to stay competitive. This revolution is just beginning, and explosive growth is inevitable.

THE SIZE OF THE B2B MARKET SPACE

Industry consultants vary in their estimates of the size of B2B e-commerce, but all of them expect B2B on-line commerce to explode as the web becomes an accepted vehicle for volume B2B purchases. Forrester Research shows that intercompany trade of hard goods over the Internet in the United States hit $43 billion in 1998. In comparison, Forrester says that the total B2C on-line commerce market was worth just $8 billion in 1998 and estimates that B2C spending on-line will be just $108 billion in 2003.

In the first edition of this book we predicted that on-exchange transactions will exceed $600 billion in value (40% of an estimated total of $1.5 trillion) by 2004 in the United States alone. Since then, the Gartner Group has predicted that global B2B e-commerce will reach $7.29 trillion by 2004 and that 37% of this will be facilitated by B2B exchanges.

Clearly, B2B Internet commerce will be enormous and could soon be as high as 70 times the size of B2C on-line commerce.

THE TECHNOLOGY OF COMMUNICATING IS NOW INVISIBLE

Previous efforts to "wire" companies together were based on EDI standards. EDI is a closed technology that costs companies hundreds of thousands of dollars to implement. Each business in an EDI network has to be linked in by dedicated connections. Every industry that wants to implement EDI to facilitate e-commerce has to start off by defining the standards that will allow one company's invoicing system to talk to another company's back-office ordering system, and then it has to build the physical connections, or dedicated network, and license the software to link those computer systems together. Every time a new supplier or customer is added to the system, the procedure has to be repeated.

In the last four years, the reliability, speed, and security of the Internet have improved to the point where more businesses are connecting to the Internet and traditional businesses are now using the Internet to conduct e-commerce and exchange information with customers, suppliers, and distributors. With the widespread adoption of Internet technologies by businesses and the acceptance of standards such as XML as the best way to exchange information online, one ubiquitous EDI mechanism is now emerging that, remarkably, requires no more than a web browser on a PC with Internet access to get connected.

Successful manufacturers are now moving away from company-unique information technology systems to more open, data-rich, flexible links with supply partners built around an Internet core.

All enterprise resource planning systems are now being modified to be both EDI compliant and fully XML capable, which also allows manufacturers committed to expensive EDI networks to connect with those suppliers who find EDI prohibitively expensive.

The issues are no longer How do we communicate? How do we build a physical connection between us? but What are we going to use this amazing new form of connectivity to do? What are the business applications that we should develop on this network?

The technology of how businesses communicate and what network businesses use is now as invisible as the wonder of electricity when we switch on the porch light.

USE OF THE INTERNET FOR SALES AND MARKETING

When businesses first start using the Internet, they tend to use it to do the same things they have done before, only cheaper, faster, and often better. Initially, the Internet has the greatest impact on businesses in the areas of sales and marketing and corporate communications through the launch of a corporate web site and adoption of e-mail.

For instance, companies take their existing brochure or catalog and put up an attractive web site, which is often referred to as "brochureware." Then they notice that they can update the web site more regularly than they used to print their catalog and that the cost of updating the web site is minimal. Then they notice that they can adjust the prices of the items listed on the web site more easily than they can change their printed catalog. Then they start to get feedback directly from customers who have visited the web site and send e-mail comments. This may be a revelation to those firms that have always sold to wholesalers or retail stores and have never really dealt with individual customers before.

In the area of corporate communications, e-mail is instantly effective in spreading information within the organization and

empowering the knowledge workers, enabling them to spend more time on strategic thinking about the company's market space, products, processes, and profitability.

As Bill Gates states in his book *Business @ the Speed of Thought: Using a Digital Nervous System,* successful companies need to have some kind of nervous system. In the new economy, it must be a digital one that ensures that information flows through the organization via e-mail, shared databases, and collaborative applications. An immediate effect of introducing the Internet into a company is that valuable information is shared more easily among and is obtained more quickly by the people in the company who need it.

HOW THE INTERNET CAN CREATE DISTRIBUTION CHANNEL CONFLICTS

Take an imaginary company that has posted its products on the Internet. One day, a bright staffer points out that the company could sell its products directly off the web site and ship them direct to the end consumer. Senior management struggles with this for a while because they realize it will upset their current distribution channels, through which they have been doing business for many years. Finally they take the plunge and start to sell directly off their web site. The company is now conducting Internet commerce. This process has already occurred in thousands of small businesses and hundreds of large businesses worldwide, including companies the size of Compaq Computer and General Motors (GM), for example.

The Internet, a simple communications tool that started out letting the company put their corporate brochure and product catalog on-line suddenly revolutionizes the company's sales and distribution system. What started out as a traditional B2B com-

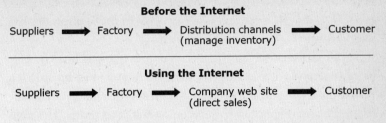

Before the Internet

Suppliers ➡ Factory ➡ Distribution channels ➡ Customer
(manage inventory)

Using the Internet

Suppliers ➡ Factory ➡ Company web site ➡ Customer
(direct sales)

HOW A TRADITIONAL B2B COMPANY CAN BECOME A B2B2C COMPANY.

pany has been transformed into a B2B2C company, simply by putting its products on-line.

This transformation is not without its shocks. The first is to the firm's existing distribution channels. Now that the firm is selling to customers directly, there is a potential conflict with its previous distribution channels. For instance, if the firm has a whole range of franchise owners, those franchise stores are going to lose sales to the web site. This potential conflict can be so enormous that it prevents the company from embracing the Internet. For example, Toys "R" Us had to abandon a proposed joint venture with Benchmark Partners that was intended to fund and launch a new on-line business operation. Apparently the venture failed because Toys "R" Us was not prepared to let the on-line business compete directly with its retail stores, since the channel conflicts would upset the managers of their existing retail stores worldwide. Similarly, now that Amway Corporation, the direct-selling business, has launched an on-line business at www.Quixtar.com, it could end up competing with its 3 million individual business owners (IBOs), who act as distributors. However, Amway has adopted an innovative approach to avoid conflicts between its new direct-sales web site and its worldwide network of IBOs, by prompting customers to enter the identification number of the IBO who referred them when making each on-line purchase. In this way the IBOs can still earn payments from the direct, on-line sales channel.

The next shock for our fictitious company comes quickly. One day they receive an order from overseas. An Internet user in Japan has visited their web site and ordered direct from them. They suddenly realize that overnight they have become a global company. The company's web site is available from anywhere in the world and is open for business 24 hours a day, 7 days a week, 365 days a year—unlike any bricks and mortar retail store. This leads to a complete rewrite of the firm's marketing strategy and customer focus. Instead of focusing exclusively on how to make their products, the company now also has to focus on how those products reach their customers and how to keep those customers happy. In other words, the manufacturer of the product is now responsible for the customer care aspects as well.

HOW THE INTERNET IS REINVENTING WORK FLOW

The above example is simplistic, but it describes the basic process that thousands of companies around the world have gone through in the last five years as a result of bringing the Internet into their business.

More recently, use of the Internet has been working a more sophisticated magic on B2B relationships. Many companies now consider the Internet crucial for procurement of goods from suppliers, management of their supply chain, and product development.

Underlying this change is a basic fundamental: The Internet is all about creating low-cost, universal communications between people, between companies, between computers run by companies, and between the assets owned by companies, with instantaneous delivery of critical information, such as the receipt of a new order, to each and every party that needs it.

In addition to computers, anything that contains a silicon chip can be connected to the network and send and receive information. That may be information as simple as whether that particular item is on or off, empty or full, hot or cold, or it may be more sophisticated information such as where it is currently located (as determined by the satellite-based Global Positioning System) and what it is doing. Whatever the information, its value to the organization can be enormous and it can totally reinvent the company's work flow.

For companies that make products, the Internet now offers the opportunity to tie together all the suppliers and shippers they deal with. The manufacturer, the suppliers, and the shippers can then track the manufacturing process from procurement through the logistics of raw-material delivery to the manufacturer and finally through to delivery of the finished product to the customer. Inventory levels, production schedules, and delivery dates are all available to everyone who needs to know. Software companies such as i2 Technologies have dedicated enormous resources to automate the supply chain management process.

Once a company integrates the Internet into everything it does at this level, it can completely reengineer its supply chain management and reinvent its whole business model.

Enabling the "build-to-order" mode

Consider the supply chain management of large manufacturers such as GM and Ford Motor Company. Car manufacturers deal with thousands of suppliers to procure all the parts (including some highly intelligent silicon chips) that now make up the average production-model car. In the past, companies like GM and Ford sought to manage all those relationships through an extremely expensive EDI-based system that tried to tie together the different computer systems that these suppliers used. The EDI system was intended to enable the manufacturer's procurement orders to be automatically accepted by the suppliers' internal systems and the suppliers' invoices to be automatically recognized and validated by the manufacturer's mainframe computers. Big parts of the expense of building the system were the costs of setting up a physical network to let these remote firms communicate with the manufacturer and licensing the software for each supplier. This meant that the car makers focused on connecting to their main suppliers (the so-called tier 1 suppliers) and left it up to them to coordinate with the myriad smaller suppliers that they relied on (tiers 2 and 3).

Companies like GM and Ford are now moving all this communication between suppliers onto the Internet. Instead of running a huge network and struggling to get systems to talk to each other, the manufacturer can now add new suppliers at any time and have a direct two-way dialog with all of the suppliers (tiers 1, 2, and 3)—a completely new way to manage supply chains.

Part of this new methodology is enabling those suppliers to post their catalog on-line for the manufacturer's procurement managers and enabling the manufacturer to run reverse auctions in which a short list of prequalified suppliers are asked to bid on a large procurement contract with the manufacturer. As we discuss in Chapter 6, the reverse-auction process can significantly reduce a company's purchase costs by making suppliers compete on price. Companies like GM and Ford claim that these new trading mechanisms have reduced their procurement costs by a staggering 25% on some items.

In Chapter 3, we explore the way in which third-party B2B exchanges are extending the role of the Internet in creating dynamic pricing models and dramatic costs savings for companies.

In a *Wall Street Journal* article on 11 August 1999, the reporter Fara Warner stated that this new network with GM's suppliers and the enhanced web sites maintained by GM (www.gm.com and www.gmbuypower.com) have enabled GM to entertain the idea of building cars to order. Of course, computer manufacturers have been doing this for several years. Michael Dell of Dell Computers has perfected the direct-sales technique and now sells more than $12 million worth of computers from www.dell.com each day (seven days a week) but waits to build each of those computers until after the order has been received.

Now imagine that you are researching your next automobile purchase on-line. You choose the various features you want from the selections on the web site and order it immediately, with your exact specifications and color preference; maybe you even apply for a loan on-line. Behind the scenes, GM does not even start building that vehicle until your order and payment (or loan) have cleared. **Less than one week later, your tailor-made car is delivered to your door.**

GM's web site enables them to communicate directly with the customer in this way. By sharing information electronically with its suppliers, GM knows when to expect the parts needed to assemble a particular car and can schedule assembly accordingly. Suppliers can tap into GM's order systems to find out what GM needs even before the parts order comes through, so they have the part ready to ship as soon as the order is placed. This creates enormous cost savings for the manufacturer by reducing the amount of parts inventory it has to hold, and it also helps ensure more on-time product deliveries. For the supplier, it removes faxed procurement orders and means that it does not have to reenter orders into its own purchasing system, since everything is integrated.

GLOBALIZATION

According to a study released by Andersen Consulting (www.ac.com), until now, most revenues from and therefore the greatest economic impact of e-commerce have been in the United States, where the e-commerce and information technology (IT) industries together account for a third of real economic growth in the past three years. Europe is rapidly eroding the U.S. lead, however. Andersen predicts that by 2002, European e-commerce revenues will equal 55% of the U.S. total. By 2003, the on-line population of the European Union is expected to match that of the United States. In a similar survey released in 1998, Andersen found that most European companies used the Internet almost exclusively for sales and marketing.

In contrast, in 1999, more than a third of the European executives surveyed by Andersen had expanded their plans, saying that they now consider the Internet crucial for the procurement of goods and services from suppliers and for logistics, finance, and product development. Fully 90% said they expect to use e-commerce in sales and marketing within five years, and 83% said they expect to use it in procurement within five years. However, most European executives acknowledged that to date, their commitment to e-commerce has lagged behind that of their U.S. counterparts.

Now that the need to spend the IT budget on Y2K fixes is over, corporate spending on integrating the Internet into everything a company does is accelerating around the world.

INTERMEDIARIES AND INFOMEDIARIES

Intermediaries who act as brokers between buyers and sellers service many B2B markets. In markets that lack price transparency and where it is difficult to find out who is buying or selling at any one point in time, the broker's role is to facilitate buyers' ability to find sellers at the right time and at a mutually acceptable price. The Chinese have a proverb that (loosely translated) states: "Big fish grow only in murky water." Applied to B2B markets, the lack of transparency in a market sometimes allows brokers to dominate the market and dictate large commission payments based on the value of the transaction, rather than on the value of the services they actually provide. In such markets, the brokers restrict the free flow of information. For example, they ensure that the prices at which trades are made are not widely disseminated and the knowledge of who is buying and selling in the market is tightly controlled.

In the securities markets, the traditional stockbrokers have controlled access to timely information about stocks. Before the Internet, unless you were able to afford to buy a terminal from an information vendor for several hundred dollars a month, the only way you could access timely stock quotes and research was through a broker. This enabled the stockbrokers to charge high commissions. Today, the Internet has enabled on-line brokers to offer stock quotes and access to research data for a fixed commission per trade at rates as low as $8 for trades that would cost more than $100 through a full-service traditional broker. Another good example of such a market is the reinsurance market, which is dominated by a few large brokers who control the flow of information between primary insurers and the underwriters at the reinsurance companies. In some reinsurance deals, commissions as high as 10% of the amount of the premium are paid to the broker who arranges the deal. Similarly, in the plastics business, middlemen reportedly charge 30% to 50% commission on some products.

In such markets, a successful B2B exchange can have the same effect as a burst of strong sunlight on a murky pond. As the sunlight burns off the algae, the water clears—buyers and sellers can identify themselves more easily, price quotes and the prices of concluded transactions start to circulate, and the market starts to become more transparent. Some brokers may therefore resist the introduction of a B2B exchange in such market spaces, although many are now recognizing the inevitability of this process and focusing on providing more value-added services to their customers.

B2B exchanges will not necessarily destroy the role of intermediaries, but they will often completely redefine it.

In fact, it is more common for the exchange to merely change the brokers' role and require them to demonstrate the value they add and charge commissions (often on a fixed-fee basis) that better reflect that value. For example, in the reinsurance world, the introduction of a B2B exchange like Catex has not precipitated the demise of the insurance brokers. Many insurers still feel more comfortable using a broker as an intermediary to handle the deal-making process—**but there is a marked trend toward lower commissions and fixed fees for consultancy services**.

In their latest book, *Net Worth,* John Hagel III (coauthor of *Net Gain*) and Marc Singer of McKinsey & Company, Inc. focus on the potential for building new business models on the Internet, rather than just doing the same things faster and cheaper. They postulate that although the Internet will result in some disintermediation, it will also enable entirely new classes of intermediary. In fact, Hagel and Singer believe that the most significant opportunities for value creation on the Internet will consist of building new kinds of intermediaries that help to shift value from vendors to customers. They call such a firm an "information intermediary," or "infomediary." Although their book is primarily focused on the potential for info-mediaries to develop between business vendors and consumers (that is, in the B2C and C2B space), Hagel and Singer's ideas can be applied to B2B markets.

In B2B markets, the B2B exchanges themselves act as a form of new infomediary, since they often empower and advance the interests of the buyer. For example, one form of B2B exchange that is developing is an infomediary who represents business buyers and aggregates their information with that of other buyers and uses the combined market power to negotiate with suppliers and seek competitive bids on their behalf. Shop2gether (www.shop2gether.com) is just such a B2B exchange with a specific focus on aggregating the purchase orders of educational institutions into collective purchases.

PROFITS ON THE INTERNET?

So far, successful B2C Internet companies have not been associated with the word "profit." Amazon.com, for example, now has a market capitalization in excess of $9 billion and claims that it stocks more than 4.7 million titles—but it has accumulated losses to end 2000 of more than $1 billion. The people who have made profits from the rapid growth of Amazon are the courier companies who distribute the books, the professional advisors who took them public, and the investors who bought early and have already sold.

eBay is an exception. It had net income of $10.8 million in 1999. But this small profit was generated on revenue of $224.7 million in that period and supports a market valuation of $18 billion.

However, analysts argue that in the new economy an Internet company's value should be based on its gross revenue, not on its

net income, and that those few B2C companies that come to dominate the Web will make monster profits in the future.

The point is that young Internet companies are often valued by their next year's forecast revenues, which demonstrate the success of their business model, market share, ability to scale up quickly, and leadership position. That basis of valuation may or may not be valid in B2C, but what is clear is that B2B e-commerce has the potential to generate substantially larger profits than B2C e-commerce.

Consider the economics of the sale of a book like this one with a ticket price of, say, $30. A common division of the spoils is as follows: author 10%, publisher 10%, wholesale distributor 50%, and retail store or Amazon.com 30%. Note that within this chain the main revenue is generated by the B2B transactions. The publishing business feeds the wholesale distributor, and takes 10% or more, and the wholesale business feeds the retail store or Amazon, and keeps 50% or more. More than 60% ($18) of the value is generated in the B2B transactions.

It follows that if Internet-based efficiencies can reduce the costs of the businesses involved in the middle of the production and supply chain, the resulting increase in profits will be greater in the B2B portion of the process than in the B2C piece (that is, the sale by the retail store to the consumer).

Translate this theoretical example to the world of B2B procurements. B2B markets where brokers use the telephone or the mail to sell products and generate commissions of 10% or more are now being targeted by B2B Internet-based exchanges. These B2B exchanges can reduce transaction costs to less than 1%, and the difference will mainly represent increased profits for the businesses and revenue for the B2B exchange.

Some of these B2B markets have enormous value. For example, each year in the United States the market for paper is worth at least

$260 billion (PaperExchange), the market for steel is $600 billion (MetalSite and e-STEEL), the market for plastics is $370 billion (PlasticsNet), and the market for reinsurance is at least $100 billion in premiums alone (Catex). Compare this with the U.S. market for books, which is just $25 billion per year. In addition, the average sticker price on most of these B2B procurement contracts is not $30, but more like $30,000, so the potential for cost savings and higher profit margins in the middle is much greater than for low-ticket consumer items like books and CDs.

CHAPTER SUMMARY

- Explosive growth in B2B markets is inevitable.
- Forrester Research shows that intercompany trade of hard goods over the Internet hit $43 billion in 1998. Gartner Group predicts that B2B Internet commerce worldwide will reach $7.29 trillion by 2004.
- Companies initially use the Internet for sales and marketing with "brochureware."
- An on-line business strategy can quickly turn a company into a B2B2C company and create channel conflicts with retail stores.
- Now companies are applying the Internet to procurement, logistics, finance, and even product development, creating a revolution in supply chain management.
- Advanced use of the Internet to contact customers and simultaneously tie together suppliers in the production process will enable customers to order products on-line—such as a customized car—and then sit back, confident that the car will be built to their specification and delivered to their door within a few days.

- B2B exchanges are challenging some market intermediaries to redefine their roles.
- B2B exchanges are creating new intermediary opportunities as a form of "infomediary."
- Profits on the Internet? Since the B2B portion of many manufacturing processes includes the majority of the value of a product, the potential cost savings and increased profits in B2B transactions are much higher than in B2C ones.

CHAPTER 3

Why B2B Exchanges Are Developing on the Internet

As we saw in Chapter 2, use of the Internet by business has so far been largely confined to sales and marketing. The first attempts at e-commerce on-line typically involved the transfer of traditional business models to the Internet.

Amazon.com is a classic example of this trend. Despite its enormous early mover advantage and popular image as an Internet innovator, Amazon.com's original business model followed the traditional distribution channels for books: production by a publisher, sales through a wholesale distributor to a retailer (albeit one selling on the Internet only), and then sales to the consumer through a centralized, physical warehouse (acting as a dispatch center for the books). Another example of an early Internet success using a classic transfer of an existing business model is Cisco Systems, which makes the "plumbing" that operates the network. Cisco sells all its routers, bridges, etc. on-line. However, new customers cannot buy from

Cisco directly on-line—they must first set up a traditional account with the company.

The innovation, to the extent that it existed, early on was in the use of the Internet to connect with existing partners to exchange information more easily (e-mail) or to move an existing product catalog onto the web for on-line sales. The price-setting mechanism for those products on-line has usually remained the same—the supplier establishes a nonnegotiable fixed price before marketing the product. For example, although Amazon.com has recently moved into the C2C auction business, it quotes a fixed price for books and CDs and has yet to let consumers bid on the retail price of its book catalog through on-line auctions. As we shall see, Amazon.com will probably take that step in the near future, at least for older titles or to clear surplus stock.

NEW B2B BUSINESS MODELS ON-LINE

The on-line business scene is now evolving at high speed, with the Internet spawning truly innovative new business models in the B2B market space. Forrester Research has identified three new models indigenous to the Internet: aggregators, auctions, and fully automated exchanges. We would add two categories: trading hubs and "post and browse." Each of these types of trading mechanism is analyzed in more detail in Chapter 6.

Aggregators. An aggregator is a one-stop shopping venue for procurement by companies. It streamlines purchasing by collecting the product catalogs of many suppliers in one place and in one format. Parts

EXAMPLES
e-Chemicals, MetalSite,
PlasticsNet

and products displayed on a single site can number in the hundreds of thousands.

Trading Hubs. These sites build buyer and seller communities for multiple verticals that have not yet embraced the Internet themselves in a specific exchange. Sellers are given virtual storefronts to advertise their products, and buyers are attracted by news, product specifications, and product reviews and recommendations. Trading hubs can be purely "horizontal," trying to support all the buyers and sellers in many different industries, or they can be "diagonal," specializing in supporting a specific type of buyer or seller or a specific type of product category across multiple industries. Trading hubs may provide an auction sale mechanism for large items with infrequent sales or an auction procurement process for aggregated small buyers.

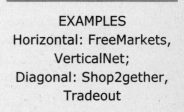

EXAMPLES
Horizontal: FreeMarkets, VerticalNet;
Diagonal: Shop2gether, Tradeout

Post and Browse Markets. A post and browse market is essentially a sophisticated bulletin board where buyers and sellers post expressions of interest to buy or sell. After "meeting" through the postings on the board, the parties negotiate a deal between themselves. The Internet enables buyers and sellers from around the world to participate on-line. This is the ideal mechanism for fragmented markets with non-standardized products, because each contract is different and requires one-on-one negotiation. These markets want to move the

EXAMPLES
BigMachines, Catex, CreditTrade, TechEx

industry toward more standardized contracts, which can then be traded in a more automated manner.

Auction Markets. The auction market is a revolutionary new pricing model for many markets in which multiple buyers or sellers bid competitively on a contract. This is the ideal mechanism for liquidating surplus at the best possible prices, since it enables a wide range of potential buyers to bid competitively for the products at below-market prices.

> EXAMPLES
> e-STEEL, Manheim Online,
> CattleOfferings

Fully Automated Exchanges. A fully automated exchange is a centralized market for standardized (or commoditylike) products. Competitive bidding between multiple buyers and sellers, with automated matching of orders, creates an efficient price-setting mechanism on-line.

> EXAMPLES
> e-STEEL, PaperExchange
> (Catex and CreditTrade are
> also moving toward this space)

In this book we focus on the development of the B2B exchanges, which include the trading hub, post and browse, auction, and fully automated exchange models.

COMMON FEATURES OF B2B EXCHANGES

B2B exchanges are similar to other exchanges that provide a neutral, centralized market space, such as stock exchanges, and share the following key advantages for on-line commerce:

- Centralized market space;
- Neutrality;
- Standardized contracts, documents, and products;
- Prequalification and regulation of the users;
- Dissemination of price quotes, posttrade information, and pricing history;
- Maintenance of the integrity of the market;
- Transparency;
- Self-regulation of the market and the pricing mechanism;
- Clearing and settlement, logistics, or other fulfillment services (including tracking of shipments);
- Integrated supply chain management;
- Product configuration;
- Confidentiality and anonymity; and
- An exchange community—a meeting place not only for members and users, but also for service providers.

In Part II of this book, we analyze these features in detail. Next we look at why the Internet allows exchanges to develop where they have not previously existed.

NET EFFECT

There are several reasons why the Internet enables exchanges to develop where they have not previously existed—and why B2B exchanges are the killer application in the B2B Internet revolution:

- Lower costs of operations: On-line markets operate at a fraction of the physical-world costs.
- Global reach: The low cost of getting connected, irrespective of geographical distance, enables fragmented buyers and sellers to find one another.
- More efficient price discovery: New dynamic price-setting mechanisms, such as on-line auctions, can improve pricing efficiency and increase volume traded.
- Process improvement: Automated trading and anonymity can eliminate many market inefficiencies, and centralized markets generate trading and pricing information (that is, transparency) that did not exist before and enable suppliers and manufacturers to integrate their internal systems to create more efficient supply chain management systems.

Challenging an entrenched market with a new B2B exchange is possible only if the new entrant can build liquidity at much lower cost. Increasingly cheap computing power and telecommunications bandwidth are what allow B2B exchanges to challenge trading floors and other traditional trading networks.

Lower costs of operation

The industrial world has created trading relationships based on three communications channels: face-to-face contact, telephone calls, and the mail. Face-to-face contacts evolved from coffee shop–style markets (for example, Lloyd's insurance market in the nineteenth century) to open outcry trading in physical pits (such as the Chicago Board of Trade [CBOT] for derivatives trading). Telephone-based markets have been improved by the use of recording machines to record the trades, fax machines to send trade confirmations, and computer screens to display indicative prices or quotes. The physical mail has progressed from the days of the pony express and the clipper ship to 24-hour delivery for most domestic destinations and only a few days for international mail. In addition, courier companies now provide guaranteed delivery of documents to almost anywhere in the world within a few days.

However, none of these methods of communication can compete with the Internet's almost instantaneous, low-cost delivery of information to any computer anywhere in the world, for both e-mail messages and web-based applications.

An on-line market does not require a physical trading floor—for which real estate is at a premium—to create a centralized market space.

Consider that the NYSE is planning to build a bigger trading floor of more than 100,000 square feet in Manhattan to house the more than six thousand floor brokers, specialists, computer technicians, and miscellaneous clerks it requires to keep the vast trading floor running smoothly. After the NYSE threatened to move to New Jersey, Rudy Giuliani, the mayor of New York City, agreed that taxpayers would pay the more than $600 million bill for this new floor. Since 1994, the NYSE has spent more than $1 billion in developing technologies that deliver orders onto the physical floor more quickly. And the CBOT has just spent $182 million to build a huge new trading floor that can house up to eight thousand traders. Combined with its existing agricultural complex, the CBOT now boasts the world's largest contiguous trading hall at 92,000 square feet, a space large enough to house two jumbo jets. Compare that with the ability of an electronic communications network (ECN), such as Archipelago Holdings, to launch, with a few small computers and for a modest cost, an Internet-based virtual trading floor that is accessible from anywhere in the world. **In fact, it is likely that the NYSE and the CBOT will no longer have physical trading floors within the next five years.**

At the CBOT, physical real estate on that expensive trading floor is at a premium, since each contract type (that is, product) has to be traded in its own physical pit—a ring or trading post where the traders gather round. This means that any new contracts that do not succeed in achieving volume quickly are removed and replaced with others. The cost of launching a new product is enormous. In 1997, the CBOT launched options and futures based on the Dow Jones Industrials Average for the first time and had to spend millions of dollars just to outfit the trading pit for the launch.

In an electronic system, the cost of adding another product to the on-line catalog or another contract to the list is almost nil. Similarly, the cost of maintaining a listing for a contract or product is very low, so new products can be given time to develop a market.

Global reach and one-stop shopping

Every day it's getting cheaper to access the Internet, and the cost of sending information by e-mail or over the web is a fraction of standard telephone, fax, and mail costs. This means that sellers can reach out to buyers all over the world and buyers can access sellers all over the world. In the physical world, businesses and individual consumers often pay a higher price for a product or buy an inferior product simply because it's the only one available in their physical location. Now

B2B exchanges can bring fragmented buyers and sellers together on the virtual trading floor of the centralized market space.

B2B exchanges create a community of buyers and sellers in a structured and organized fashion. After participants view the offers posted on the exchange, communications between potential buyers and sellers are targeted specifically to the interested parties. The on-line exchange thus generates great sales leads to prequalified buyers. Unlike general e-mail on the Internet, communications through a central exchange can be organized, encrypted, authenticated, time-stamped, tracked, and verified.

The low cost of getting connected, irrespective of geographical distance, enables fragmented buyers and sellers to find each other through a B2B exchange without incurring real-world search and travel expenses or high commissions for using intermediaries. In addition, by aggregating multiple sellers in one place, an exchange creates a one-stop shopping experience for buyers. This will force traditional intermediaries, such as brokers, to redefine their roles in B2B markets but will create new opportunities for "infomediaries," as discussed in Chapter 2.

More efficient price discovery

In the industrial economy, most prices are set by the seller, who generally has more economic power than the buyer and can publish a catalog with nonnegotiable prices. An alternative method is to bring together all the potential buy and sell orders at any particular time and let competing offers set the highest price or the price that maximizes the amount sold. That price can truly be called the market price at that particular point in time.

Dynamic pricing through competitive bidding and auction systems is one of the most exciting features of B2B exchanges

and, as we shall explore in Chapter 6, a key component of the revolutionary nature of B2B Internet commerce.

Auction pricing is the approach adopted by ECNs with their central market matching systems for securities. It is also the price discovery mechanism eBay adopted to run its on-line markets. Increasingly, it is the price-setting mechanism being used by many B2B exchanges, as the Internet can bring together bids and offers from all over the world with its ability to interconnect companies cheaply.

As with securities markets, the more competing buyers and sellers that can be brought together, the more liquid the market becomes and the more efficient the price-setting mechanism is.

For example, in the U.S. securities industry, ECNs are creating more efficient order execution and pricing than are traditional stock exchanges like Nasdaq (National Association of Securities Dealers' Automated Quotations) and the NYSE. Nasdaq has been particularly affected by ECNs, starting with the success of Instinet (a Reuters company) and now the launch of approximately fifty proprietary trading systems, around ten of which have been approved by the SEC as ECNs. This is because Nasdaq operates a "quotation" system whereby market-makers make quotes to buy or sell a security and a consumer's order is executed against the market-makers' prices. Market-makers ensure that there is a gap between the "bid" (the buy price) and the "ask" (the sell price) so they make a profit on each trade. This gap is known as the "spread" and is a hidden cost of dealing on Nasdaq, because consumers' orders are matched not at the best price each is willing to pay but at the prices set by the market-maker. This hidden cost is justified if there is low liquidity in a particular stock, because the market-maker is adding value by ensuring that there are always bid and ask prices, even if there are not two consumers looking to buy and sell at that time.

Nasdaq was developed to trade small capitalization stocks that could not be listed on the NYSE and were generally illiquid. As some of the companies on Nasdaq, such as Microsoft and Dell Computers, grew, Nasdaq became much more liquid, and the "blue-chip" stocks naturally no longer required market-makers. However, the market-makers blocked development of a central matching engine (called a "central limit order book") at Nasdaq that would allow consumers' orders to be matched directly at a single price. In fact, an SEC investigation in the mid-1990s discovered that many market-makers were also colluding to fix the spreads in some stocks. Consequently, in January 1997 the SEC introduced new order handling rules that require market-makers to trade at the price specified by the customer if they have buy and sell orders at the same price.

This has enabled ECNs to step into the market and offer central limit order books that match orders at the best price, that is, the price at which the buyer and seller have indicated they are willing to trade. Any order that cannot be matched in the ECN's order book is routed to Nasdaq for execution against a market-maker. The problem for Nasdaq is that these ECNs are effectively sucking liquidity out of the exchange and leaving the market-makers with only those trades that cannot be filled quickly by the ECN. From the consumer's point of view, the ECNs have created a more efficient mechanism for matching orders and thus reduced their trading costs. This has enabled ECNs to attract more than 25% of Nasdaq's trading volume away from the exchange on a daily basis.

More transparency

Most markets operate with imperfect information about prices of similar deals or supply and demand. Once a centralized exchange develops, the pricing, volumes, and trading history become available to all users in a way that was not possible before.

The traditional world of B2B reinsurance is a good example. In the past, primary insurers obtained reinsurance quotes from wholesale reinsurers through an insurance broker. The broker would cultivate relationships with several key reinsurers (or "markets") to obtain the best quotes for the primary insurer and the best commissions for the broker. To protect their markets, the brokers do not share the pricing information among themselves or among their clients, so there is no transparency in the pricing process. Primary insurers do not know what other companies are paying for reinsurance. By controlling that information, the brokers have been able to charge commissions of up to 10% on multimillion-dollar premiums.

Now that Catex has established a B2B exchange for insurance products, the price at which reinsurance contracts are executed through their system is immediately broadcast on the Internet to all registered users. But every trade report is fully anonymous, so that other users do not know who the contract parties are. Although brokers are still used in the system, they give up the confidentiality regarding the pricing of their deals and, in return, obtain the pricing information from their competitors' deals. This price transparency ensures that the market becomes deeper and more liquid. Partly as a result of Catex—and partly as a result of the other dynamics of the new economy—the broker's role in the insurance world is rapidly changing. Brokers now provide more value-added services (such as analytical functions, consulting, and clearing) in return for fixed fees as opposed to the large commissions of the past.

PaperExchange is bringing the same price transparency to another industry in which brokers are relied on heavily and neither the seller nor the buyer really knows what a central market price should be. PaperExchange permits buyers and sellers of paper products of all grades and sizes to post expressions of interest to buy or sell at quoted prices. Buyers or sellers can then post counteroffers until a contract price is reached. All price quotes are openly published on the web site.

Similarly, exchanges enable buyers and sellers to gauge supply and demand at any time. The orders, or expressions of interest, that are posted at the exchange indicate how much people want to buy and sell and may also indicate who is buying or selling.

A B2B exchange can thus generate transparency regarding pricing and the level of supply and demand in the market at any particular point in time.

Removing market inefficiencies

As well as expanding markets geographically, B2B exchanges can remove market inefficiencies. For example, in the securities markets one major inefficiency is what institutions call "market impact." This phenomenon occurs when information about a large buy or sell order leaks into the market and causes the price to move dramatically against the party trying to buy or sell. Leaks can happen when brokers, market-makers, or specialist firms are used. Studies by securities analysts such as SEI Investments show that the largest transaction cost for an institution may be not the commission or a market-maker's spread, but this market impact as other traders react to news about block trades by moving market prices. On the other hand, anonymity allows institutional investors to sell large blocks of a stock without fear that buyers will vanish and prices will fall sharply as word leaks out that the smart money is selling.

The electronic trading systems the ECNs are now offering and B2B exchanges are adopting can provide total anonymity for traders and thus remove market impact.

Instinet, the Reuters-owned electronic marketplace, has been able to attract up to 20% of Nasdaq's daily volume, largely as a result of its widely advertised anonymity and its ability to avoid market impact. In addition, sophisticated trading systems can allow traders to enter a large order but disclose only a fraction of the volume to the market. As a visible order gets matched, the electronic system automatically feeds the remaining volume into the order book in preset amounts. Again, this enables a large order to be executed with minimum market impact.

Outside of the securities industry there are plenty of existing supply chains that involve too many intermediaries, which creates inefficiencies. The National Transportation Exchange (NTE), for example, has been very successful in selling empty capacity on returning trucks to suppliers who previously had no way of accessing that haulage capacity. The suppliers get cut-price deals and the trucking companies get to sell previously unused back-haul space. NTE's web site (www.nte.net) states that it "provides a real-time, neutral platform for Member shippers who tender loads, as well as the direct service carrier Members, which tender the available space capacity of their moving trucks. NTE has named its service 'The Exchange' because it enables its Members to conduct profitable business together, through a real-time marketplace setting, just like a stock exchange. Also, like a stock exchange, it has defined processes, data capture and reporting, open accessibility for its Members, interfaces to other needed technologies, and even processes transportation billing and payment with third party oversight."

More efficient management of supply chains

Net markets have a unique capability to unite the manufacturer with its suppliers (tier 1) and its suppliers' suppliers (tiers 2 and 3). This can lead to dramatic reductions in manufacturing time by facilitating just-in-time delivery of parts, reducing inventory levels at all stages.

Linkages between multiple suppliers and manufacturers create intelligent routing of orders to the supplier with the right capacity and allow for more efficient logistical distribution. Deep electronic linkages with a manufacturer's suppliers can also dramatically accelerate the new product design process, since the suppliers can directly input into the process in real time.

VERTICAL KNOWLEDGE

B2B exchanges are being developed by consortia of established bricks and mortar buyers and sellers and by experienced vertical industry professionals who, having seen businesses adopt Internet technologies, recognize an enormous opportunity to leave their Industrial Age corporations and start up a B2B exchange. These professionals and industry consortia have deep knowledge of their particular industry and strong relationships with the main buyers and sellers in that vertical space.

This vertical knowledge is critical to an exchange if it is to build credibility quickly and be customized for that particular market.

CHANNEL CONFLICTS FOR MANUFACTURERS

As we saw in Chapter 2, manufacturers who start to offer their products for sale on-line can create enormous conflicts with their traditional distribution channels, which were developed to achieve maximum distribution of the manufacturers' products in a pre-Internet environment. The distribution channels also help manufacturers manage and store inventory of completed products in return for a percentage of the sales price. Manufacturers whose loyalty to their traditional distribution channels keeps them from selling on-line may offer enormous potential for an independent third party to provide a neutral sales mechanism on-line.

B2B exchanges are the neutral third-party market spaces that enable all manufacturers to change the way they sell their products, without having to compete with their existing distribution channels.

Even when manufacturers are able to put up their own on-line storefront to sell directly, they will find that a B2B exchange is more attractive to many buyers. This is because a neutral third-party exchange posts the storefronts of multiple manufacturers in one place, facilitating the buyer's search for the best product at the best price.

IMPACT OF B2B EXCHANGES

B2B exchanges are already having a dynamic impact on traditional markets. The effects are bound to multiply, like ripples in a pond, since this revolution is only just beginning. The main effects we have observed so far are

- Lower costs;
- Higher potential profits for manufacturers who lower their procurement costs;
- Increased depth and liquidity in a market;
- Lower inventory requirements;
- Greater transparency and more orderly markets;
- Elimination of geographical barriers and time zone differences;
- Tighter integration of purchasing systems;
- Improved product design schedules through integration with suppliers; and
- Removal of distribution channel blockages, such as agents and brokers who have a lock on a particular market, resulting in a potential loss of jobs or changes in the nature of the role of traditional intermediaries.

A WHO'S WHO OF B2BS

Four years ago there were no on-line B2B exchanges outside of the securities markets. Today there are around one thousand. In the Appendix we give detailed profiles of the leading B2B exchanges that we have studied:

BigMachines (www.bigmachines.com)—industrial machinery
Catex (www.catex.com)—insurance markets
CreditTrade (www.credittrade.com)—credit derivatives
e-Chemicals (www.e-chemicals.com)—industrial chemicals
e-STEEL (www.esteel.com)—steel and other metals
MetalSite (www.metalsite.net)—steel and other metals
NTE (www.nte.net)—trucking
PaperExchange (www.paperexchange.com)—paper
PlasticsNet (www.plasticsnet.com)—plastics
TechEx (www.techex.com)—life sciences intellectual property

CHAPTER SUMMARY

- Early e-commerce was dominated by attempts to move traditional business models on-line.
- The Internet has spawned five new business models: aggregators, trading hubs, post and browse, auction markets, and fully automated exchanges.
- Each model is rapidly redefining business strategies and trade flows.
- B2B exchanges are the killer application because they allow lower operating costs, global reach, dynamic pricing, and process improvement.

- B2B exchanges remove market inefficiencies and rapidly expand markets geographically. For example, in the securities arena, ECNs are developing to create more efficient order execution away from traditional stock exchanges.

- Challenging an entrenched market with a new B2B exchange is possible only if the new entrant can build liquidity at much lower cost. Increasingly cheap computing power and telecommunications bandwidth allow B2B exchanges to challenge trading floors and other traditional trading networks.

- The low cost of getting connected, irrespective of geographical distance, enables fragmented buyers and sellers to find each other through a B2B exchange without incurring real-world search and travel expenses or high commissions for using intermediaries.

- Vertical knowledge is critical to an exchange if it is to build credibility quickly and suit its particular market.

- Leading examples of B2B exchanges are BigMachines, Catex, e-STEEL, MetalSite, PaperExchange, CreditTrade, TechEx, PaperExchange, PlasticsNet, and NTE.

CHAPTER 4

"It's NOT the Technology, Stupid!"

Although it is the Internet's technology that makes business-to-business exchanges possible, the exchanges themselves are primarily business applications and not technological innovations. The real long-term value of a B2B exchange to its users is greatly enhanced if the exchange is tailor-made for the specific market in which it operates—and this requires the exchange to be designed primarily from a business perspective rather than a purely technological one.

Internet and web browser-based technologies are now ubiquitous, so the value of an exchange must come from its market-specific design and business solutions.

CUSTOMIZING THE EXCHANGE'S OFFERING

In the physical world, successful exchanges focus on a specific area. For example, in the securities industry the Nasdaq exchange has thrived despite the strength of the NYSE, because it specializes in listing smaller capitalization and high-growth technology stocks that are not so welcome on the "Big Board" at the NYSE. Similarly, physical markets are tailored for their users and do not mix different products into the same program. For example, a cattle auction is held at a location that facilitates the delivery, storage, and display of cattle and is held at a time suitable for farmers; a secondhand car auction is held at a different facility and is designed specifically for car dealers.

The on-line world is no different. Users want to log onto a site designed just for them and their market, so they can get the information or products they want as quickly as possible.

Take a look at Manheim (www.manheim.com) and their Cyber-Lot Demo, which is an on-line secondhand car auction. The site is designed specifically for car dealers and does not include other products. Similarly, CattleOfferings.com caters to livestock sales and agribusiness. The point is to create a community that has a look, feel, and functionality that any specialized users recognize immediately. Equally important, it has to be easy to use and have low barriers to entry, that is, no new hardware, proprietary software, or other up-front costs. Fortunately, the Network, based on Internet technologies with widespread connectivity, allows you to do this in the new economy.

SECURING A CRITICAL MASS OF USERS

To kick-start the laws of increasing returns, an exchange must build up the number of buyers and sellers who use its market space as quickly as possible. Many industries are slow to change ingrained practices. Therefore, some B2B exchanges form partnerships with companies that can help migrate market-makers in an evolutionary way rather than expect the change to happen overnight. A good example of this is the partnership that CreditTrade, the credit trading exchange, formed with Prebon Yamane, a leading credit derivatives voice brokerage. Under the agreement, Prebon Yamane moved its global credit derivatives team and historical default swap database to CreditTrade in return for a substantial equity stake. In all, 13 credit derivatives brokers in London, New York, and Singapore joined Credit-Trade's online credit sales desk to form a single global team. The agreement highlights the potential to use the personal attention provided by traditional voice brokers to accelerate the market's acceptance of the speed, efficiency, and cost-effectiveness of an Internet exchange.

Establishing a critical mass of users is far more important to the ultimate success of the exchange than having the most advanced technology.

USING OPEN, INTERNET-BASED SYSTEMS

The main technology being adopted by B2B exchanges is systems based on Transmission Control Protocol/Internet Protocol and standards like Extensible Markup Language (XML) as the common protocol to define data. Use of this standard enables you to build on the Internet and browser-based applications that are now ubiquitous. It is not advisable to spend any money building a closed proprietary system, even if you think that locking users into your system will protect you from competition—that is the cul-de-sac that EDI drove into.

A good example of the Internet's power is the Catex (www.catex. com) insurance risk B2B exchange. Version 1 of the Catex trading and information application was built as a proprietary system using Windows NT 4.0 and required each user to have a dedicated connection, or dial-up access, to the exchange's servers. In November 1998, the exchange launched Version 2 as an open, web-based application; immediately the system was available to any preauthorized executive with a web browser on a PC with Internet access. Demonstrating the system became a simple matter: Instead of lugging around a heavy laptop containing a demo of the Version 1 system, a customer representative could pull up the system on the client's desktop and show the live version. The sign-up of new subscribers has grown exponentially since Catex switched to its Internet system. "It has had a dramatic impact," says Frank Fortunato, the CEO of Catex, in an article in *Insurance Networking*. "We can deliver the product much more quickly." Anyone with Internet access and a valid user ID and password can now access the live Catex trading system on-line.

Security worries have largely been removed on the Internet with the use of user names and passwords to restrict access and standard encryption methods to protect confidential information passing over the open net. Also, in the B2B market space, exchanges are able to offer authentication and tracking services for communications through an exchange's infrastructure; anonymity, where applicable, and digital signatures to sign and secure digital documents.

OUTSOURCING THE TECHNOLOGY

Throughout this book we advise the builders of B2B exchanges to outsource their technology development. **It is critical for a successful B2B exchange to focus on its core competency—the specific industry expertise that will enable it to create the best business solution possible for that market—and let the outside technology experts build the system.** A good example is the e-STEEL exchange, which partnered right from the start with Computer Sciences Corporation (www.CSC.com) to build its trading system. This left the management of e-STEEL free to work with the steel industry to market the exchange and get user input on the system's design.

For three years, B2B exchanges had to build their own systems, because third-party options were not available. In the last two years, a rash of startups and some established companies have rushed to build and sell the technology for on-line auctions and other exchange functions. Prominent among them are Ariba, Commerce One, i2 Technologies, Moai Technologies and RightWorks. As the B2B exchange market space expands, the traditional software companies are sure to expand their offerings in this area. For example, IBM already has a suite of e-commerce products, and Microsoft has moved into the on-line auction space with an auction tool kit for its Site Server Commerce software. In addition, some of the specialist stock exchange system vendors, such as Computershare, EFA Software, OptiMark Technologies, and OM Systems, are now seeing the opportunity to refocus their industrial-strength trading and matching engines on B2B exchange applications.

Indeed, many opportunities have been spawned by the growth of B2B exchanges, such as providing technology, marketing, connectivity, content and data services, and consulting to these new companies. Forrester Research projects that the overall market for just the software that facilitates e-commerce could reach nearly $500 million by 2003.

GOING IN WITH INDUSTRY EXPERTISE— VERTICAL KNOWLEDGE

B2B exchanges need the highest level of industry-specific expertise to gain widespread credibility quickly within their chosen market space. It is the kiss of death for a startup exchange to be told to talk to a potential member's information technology (IT) staff rather than the senior business people, traders, CFO, and CEO. The B2B exchange is a business solution that requires the full endorsement of a company's top management and not just the approval of its technology staff. This is particularly true for an exchange that creates a paradigm shift in the way business is done in that market space. In many cases, there is a disconnect between IT and business leaders in perception of the strategic direction of the company.

PaperExchange is chaired by Roger Stone, one of the leading luminaries of the paper industry. Stone built the Stone Container Corporation into a $7.8 billion revenue company prior to its merger with Jefferson Smurfit in late 1998. Stone Container was the largest containerboard and packaging company in the world, with 43,000 employees and operations in more than 50 countries. In a press release Jason Weiss, the CEO of PaperExchange, stated, "Every CEO of every paper mill in the world knows Roger Stone and will meet with him. . . . He'll make the mills feel comfortable with us and know that we're going to help the industry."

Frank Fortunato and Frank Sweeney, who between them have many years of experience as attorneys in the insurance industry, conceived of the Catastrophe Risk Exchange, or Catex. Because of their credibility within the industry, Fortunato and Sweeney were able to get U.S. insurance companies to work closely with them from the inception of the exchange. This collaboration led to many ideas for design features and industry-specific functions that the technology team might have overlooked.

CREATING HORIZONTAL TRADING HUBS

Prominent in this space are existing trading hubs such as VerticalNet (www.verticalnet.com) and FreeMarkets (www.freemarkets.com). These sites build buyer and seller communities for specific industries that have not yet embraced the Internet. Sellers are given virtual storefronts to advertise their products, and buyers are attracted by news, product specifications, and product reviews and recommendations. Trading hubs are moving to provide auction sale mechanisms, especially for large items with infrequent sales. For example, Vertical-Net has auctioned three power plants in their "poweronline" vertical.

We call this model a "horizontal trading hub," because the companies offer similar applications and support all the buyers and sellers across diverse industries (or verticals). For example, VerticalNet currently operates 57 vertical communities grouped into sectors such as advanced technologies, communications, environmental, food and packaging, food service/hospitality, healthcare, manufacturing and metals, science, and services.

One issue sure to arise with this type of service is whether a one-size-fits-all model can succeed in the B2B exchange market space. We believe that only industry-specific sites will thrive and be adopted throughout an industry. Once a community has developed in a horizontal trading hub, it may migrate to a B2B exchange that is run by experts with specialist knowledge in that vertical and is tailored to that market. In such cases the horizontal trading hubs become catalysts or incubators for subsequent specialist B2B exchanges.

Horizontal trading hubs will flourish in niche areas where a company deals only infrequently, such as auctioning last year's fashions or other excess inventory, and therefore will not have enough critical mass to support an industry-specific site.

CREATING DIAGONAL TRADING HUBS

"Diagonal trading hubs" support a specific type of buyer or seller or support a specific type of product category across multiple industries.

Prominent in this area is Tradeout (www.tradeout.com), a specialist trading hub where businesses liquidate surplus inventory and idle assets, a marketplace that Tradeout estimates is worth more than $300 billion per year. Currently, excess inventory and idle assets are sold globally through a variety of inefficient distribution channels. Sellers get prices below fair market value, and buyers frequently cannot locate items they want when they want them. Tradeout is trying to reduce this inefficiency by providing a central Internet-based B2B exchange where a universe of buyers and sellers can connect on-line. Tradeout sells items in more than 50 product categories in an auction-based, sealed-bid, or fixed-price format.

Another diagonal trading hub is eScout (www.escout.com), which enables small business buyers to aggregate their orders into one larger order that is then bid for by multiple sellers. eScout does not focus on a specific industry or vertical; rather, it serves the small business buyer in multiple verticals—in effect, the small business buyer is the vertical.

Diagonal trading hubs are likely to be highly successful, because they provide a specific service tailored to a particular type of buyer or seller.

CHAPTER SUMMARY

- B2B exchanges are business applications, not information technology applications.
- The Internet and web browser-based technologies are now ubiquitous, so the value of an exchange must come from the market-specific design and business solution.
- Do not build a proprietary model (for example, Catex Version 1.0); use the Internet (Catex Version 2.0).
- Outsource the technology (for example, e-STEEL).
- Companies such as Ariba and Commerce One (auction markets) now sell the core technologies.

- B2B exchanges need a high level of industry-specific expertise and credibility so they can get in to see the CFO or CEO of potential members and do not get told to speak to the information technology people.
- Horizontal trading hubs and technology initiatives, which attempt to build B2B trading networks for many different industries may just become incubators for specialized B2B exchanges in each vertical unless they specialize in a niche (for example, auctioning off excess inventory), which does not happen frequently.
- Diagonal trading hubs, which focus on a specific type of buyer or seller, or a specific product category across multiple markets, should be very successful.

Part II

ANATOMY OF A B2B EXCHANGE

CHAPTER 5

Membership and Ownership Models

As we explained in Chapter 1, what is unique about an exchange is that it brings many buyers and sellers together in a central market space and enables them to buy and sell from each other at a price that is determined in accordance with the rules of the exchange. Since an exchange represents *many* buyers and sellers—in a many-to-many model—the way to build a successful B2B exchange is different from how a standard B2B e-commerce company is built.

In particular, an exchange must remain neutral and balance the competing interests of all its users. Providing an open, fair, and transparent market is essential to an exchange's value proposition and enhances its ability to attract business.

B2B exchanges will have some or all of the following user groups, many of whom will have different objectives or interests:

- Owners—that is, the shareholders;
- Sellers or suppliers;
- Buyers or procuring companies;

- Brokers or other forms of intermediaries/infomediaries;
- Listed companies (such as for stock exchanges);
- Issuers of traded products (for example, securitized contracts);
- Data vendors and service providers;
- The general public;
- The government.

THE CONCEPT OF MEMBERSHIP

Since an exchange has multiple buyers and sellers accessing its trading systems, it must have some form of membership structure to determine who is permitted to have access and what type of access they will have to the central market space.

The membership structure may be as simple as a subscription agreement that a potential user must complete to sign on—in the same way new consumers can simply sign on to eBay to trade in their on-line C2C auctions. At the other end of the scale, the membership criteria may include a full set of trading membership rules and trading regulations, which require new members to be prevetted and approved by the exchange. In such cases, the rules lay out the steps to becoming a member and the obligations, ongoing compliance requirements, and system requirements expected of members.

The initial criteria for obtaining membership of the exchange usually cover

- Whether the firm is fit and proper;
- Relevant experience of the staff;
- The creditworthiness of the firm;
- The firm's capital;
- Proper regulatory controls within the firm.

Regulating who has access to the market and how they can operate within the market is also a key element of a B2B exchange's value proposition. For example, CreditTrade.com restricts trading access to prevetted financial institutions. To sign up as a trader, you must fill out forms on the web site and then await the receipt of your user name and password, following the due diligence checks carried out by the exchange.

Stock exchanges are one of the oldest forms of formalized central markets. The first stock exchange was founded in Amsterdam in 1611. Over the years, stock exchanges have developed and refined several membership models. Our experience in dealing with traditional stock exchanges provides some important lessons in understanding the potential membership and ownership models for B2B exchanges.

THE FOUR STANDARD MODELS OF EXCHANGE MEMBERSHIP AND OWNERSHIP

There are four common membership and ownership structures for exchanges:

- Ownership by one group of users, with closed membership;
- Ownership by many user groups, with open membership;
- Ownership by one or more commercial investors, with open membership;
- Ownership by government.

Ownership by one group of users, with closed membership

An exchange may be owned and controlled by one group of users, for example, the traders or brokers who act for buyers and sellers in the market. In this model, new trading members are required to buy an ownership stake, often referred to as a "seat," in the exchange.

The strength of this model is that the ownership group can design the market to their advantage and profit. In particular, they can control membership by restricting who can buy a seat or limiting the number of seats available (thus ensuring that a seat appreciates in value!). The biggest problem is that all other user groups may be disadvantaged by the owners' anticompetitive practices.

The World Insurance Network (www.worldins.com) was an exchange owned exclusively by one group of users who kept the membership closed. A consortium of the largest insurance brokers set up this company in 1995 to provide e-commerce facilities to insurance and reinsurance companies. Although they spent millions of dollars on building a proprietary Electronic Data Interchange (EDI) product, the service never achieved widespread acceptance, because it was owned and controlled by six insurance brokers—who have since merged to become three large firms. Having designed EDI standards and built physical networks for insurance players to communicate with one another, the World Insurance Network promptly discovered that the advent of the Internet brought one common standard and communication is no longer the issue. The company then merged with two other EDI-based solutions, RINET and LIMNET, and was renamed WISe, for Worldwide Insurance e-commerce. WISe, however, is still constrained from becoming a true B2B exchange because it is owned by brokers and the largest insurance companies, and those owners do not want WISe to compete with them in their present business space.

As the digital economy develops, intermediaries in all markets affected by the B2B revolution will no doubt be tempted to set up their own exchange to try and protect their market position. However, as we shall show, broker-owned exchanges are no longer viable in the face of the open competition made possible by the Internet.

Examples from the securities market

Most old stock exchanges, such as the New York, London, and Toronto Stock Exchanges, were set up by stockbrokers and are still owned exclusively by the brokers. Such exchanges operate rather like a "mutual society" or private club.

The NYSE is an example of what can happen when an exchange is owned by one group of users (in this case, the broker members). The original "Buttonwood Tree" Agreement (named after a buttonwood tree at 68 Wall Street under which the brokers met) that formally constituted the NYSE on 17 May 1792 states as follows:

> We the subscribers, brokers for the purchase and sale of public stock do hereby solemnly promise and pledge ourselves to each other, that we will not buy or sell from this day on for any persons what-so-ever any kind of public stock at less rate than one-quarter percent commission on the special value of, and that we give preference to each other in our negotiations.

So the brokers sought to exclude other traders and control the prices at which stocks were bought and sold, and particularly, the price of the commissions charged by the brokers for trading on behalf of a client. A fixed commission structure effectively prevents the brokers from competing on price and denies the investing public the economic benefits of competitive market forces. In the United Kingdom the practice of imposing minimum fixed-scale fees was cited as an anticompetitive restriction in an antitrust case brought against the London Stock Exchange under the Restrictive Trade Practices Act of 1976. The fact that the NYSE acted as a private club played a part in the U.S. government's passing the Securities Exchange Act of 1934, which requires all national securities markets to be registered by the SEC. However, it was not until 1975 that the SEC finally forced the NYSE to give up its fixed commission structure. Some broker-owned stock exchanges, including the Stock Exchange of Hong Kong, still maintain fixed commissions.

Other forms of restrictive practice that are commonly carried on by a broker-owned exchange include

- A closed system, not allowing "remote" members to have access (for example, the Stock Exchange of Hong Kong);
- Restrictions on the number of terminals or of branches or offices that a member can have (for example, the Stock Exchange of Hong Kong);
- Restrictions on how many shares or seats a member can own (for example, the NYSE);
- Weighted voting rights or restrictions on how many votes certain types of members can have (for example, the Chicago Board of Trade).

In the 1970s, after dramatic declines in revenues, membership (a 33% decline between 1968 and 1972), and the value of its seats, the NYSE embarked on a decade of adjustments to its practices and governance. Partly on its own initiative and partly in response to pressures from the SEC, the NYSE introduced changes in its trading procedures, including limited automation, admission of "access" members who were not required to have an ownership stake, and removal of the fixed commission structure. The board was reduced from 33 to 21 members, the majority of whom are now drawn from the public rather than from member firms, and industry representation on the board was also revised. Key management roles such as chairman, CEO, and COO were turned over to professionals outside of NYSE membership.

In the digital revolution that is creating the new economy, the NYSE has faced new and increasing competition from electronic communications networks (ECNs).

These electronic trading systems enable orders to bypass the NYSE and Nasdaq and be matched in a central limit order book. Faced with the threat of these new hybrid exchanges, the NYSE claims that it cannot compete without further capital (even though it has already spent more than $1 billion on technology since 1994). The NYSE now proposes to demutualize, which involves a transformation from a broker-owned association into a for-profit company, and to file for its own IPO.

In the last 20 years, as the anticompetitive features of broker-owned stock exchanges have become increasingly unacceptable, governments all over the world have sought to make these exchanges more representative of the wider public interest. As with the NYSE, the most common approach has been to require the governing body of the exchange to include a number of nonbroker representatives. Sometimes, the government insists on appointing government representatives. In the last five years, competitive pressures from electronic trading systems have forced all broker-owned exchanges to consider demutualization to become for-profit entities with all restrictive practices removed. The Bermuda Stock Exchange (BSX) demutualized in 1992, and the Stockholm Stock Exchange (SSE) demutualized and went public in 1993. The Australian Stock Exchange went public in 1998, followed by the London Stock Exchange in early 2000. Now the NYSE, Nasdaq, and Toronto Stock Exchanges are all talking about going public.

Ownership by many users, with open membership

An alternative approach is to start with wider ownership, representing all of the users of the exchange. In this model, the application for membership, or ability to trade on the exchange, is not linked to an ownership stake and new memberships are on a nondiscriminatory basis. A member does not have to own a seat, but needs a license to trade on the exchange and use its facilities. This license may be transferable by a member, or the exchange may insist that new members join the exchange directly so that membership rights are nontransferable.

The advantage of this approach is the ability to balance the competing interests of each user group. The disadvantage is that it can take a long time to get all these potentially disparate groups to work together.

Examples from the securities market

The open membership model has been adopted in many newer stock exchanges (particularly in emerging markets, which have the benefit of starting with a clean sheet). In the last ten years, most new stock exchanges have been set up by nonbrokers, with the investors opening up trading membership of the exchange to everyone who meets the requirements of the exchange. The following exchanges are examples of the open membership model:

The Bermuda Stock Exchange (BSX). The BSX was demutualized in 1992 by the creation of a for-profit company. Membership was opened up and detached from ownership.

The Luxembourg Stock Exchange. The exchange is a public company with wide share ownership that distributes surpluses to shareholders as dividends.

The National Stock Exchange of India (NSE). Owned by a group of financial institutions, the NSE was set up with the blessing of the Indian government to counteract the anticompetitive practices adopted by the Bombay Stock Exchange. By implementing a fully electronic dealing system with equal access (by way of satellite-linked terminals) from all the main cities, the NSE surpassed Bombay as the leading stock exchange in India, by volume, within 18 months of its launch.

The Stockholm Stock Exchange (SSE). Demutualized in 1993, the SSE was owned by many user groups until 1998, when the OM Gruppen purchased it.

The SSE is an interesting example of open membership. In 1993, the SSE transformed itself from a traditional broker-owned exchange into a public company owned equally by the broker members and the listed companies. Shares in the Stockholm Exchange Company were then made available for members of the public to buy. The move to privatized ownership was seen as particularly important to achieving faster decision making and more effective response to the market. The SSE's first act as a private company was to allow remote membership and direct execution of orders from other cities.

These strategic initiatives have succeeded by almost every measure. The market has flourished, with market capitalization increasing five times and trading volumes increasing twenty times since 1990. Trading fees have been cut by more than half and entry fees by two-thirds. The SSE has also attracted more liquidity. In fact, 90% of companies interlisted on the NYSE now trade 90% of their volume in Stockholm. The SSE has also succeeded in expanding its international presence, since many members trade remotely, and became the first stock exchange to receive the coveted ISO 9001 certification.

In 1998, the OM Gruppen, which operated several securities exchanges, including a traded options market called OM Stockholm, bought the SSE. On 1 July 1999, the SSE and OM Stockholm merged to establish the OM Stockholm Exchange, combining their activities in this newly incorporated entity.

Ownership by one or more benign commercial investors, with open membership

In this model, the exchange is set up and operated by one benign investor or a group of investors and is run totally on a for-profit basis. Membership, or the ability to trade on the exchange, is not linked to ownership, and new memberships are available to applicants on an open-access, nondiscriminatory basis without the requirement to purchase a seat.

Ownership by an investor, with open membership, has been the most prevalent model in the establishment of B2B exchanges in the last four years. Good examples are Catex, CreditTrade, e-Chemicals, PaperExchange, PlasticsNet, National Transportation Exchange, and TechEx.

PlasticsNet's story is typical of the funding histories of many independent, third-party B2B exchanges. In early 1994, Tim and Nick Stojka discovered a way that the Internet could be used to streamline the supply chain processes in the plastics industry, and they began to explore the concept for PlasticsNet. Sons of the founder of Fast Heat, a supplier to the plastics industry, the Stojka brothers grew up in the plastics business and understood industry practices. They also recognized the problems the Internet could solve. Based in Chicago, the brothers established CommerX (www.commerx.com) as a private company and launched PlasticsNet (www.plasticsnet.com) in September 1995.

PlasticsNet was initially funded by CommerX as a benign commercial investor. A second round of fundraising attracted financing from the Internet Capital Group, and PlasticsNet is now engaged in a third round of financing. The brothers now claim that PlasticsNet's site is the first electronic commerce center for the $390 billion per annum U.S. plastics industry. Since March 1999, the site has evolved from a trade community and sourcing guide for the plastics industry into a fully fledged marketplace with complete e-commerce capabilities. CommerX is now in the process of establishing similar exchanges in other related vertical spaces.

Examples from the securities market

In the securities market, the following are the best examples of exchanges owned by benign commercial investors, with open membership:

Instinet. Instinet is the largest and oldest ECN in the United States and is wholly owned by Reuters PLC. It provides anonymous order matching.

The Arizona Stock Exchange (www.azx.com). This electronic auction market was set up and is run by a group of private investors.

Tradepoint Stock Exchange (www.tradepoint.co.uk). This electronic dealing system was set up in London by a group of private investors, was listed on the Vancouver Stock Exchange, and is now owned by a consortium of large broker-dealers, including Morgan Stanley, JP Morgan and Instinet, and the Archipelago ECN. Tradepoint currently trades U.K. equities but is in the process of becoming a pan-European ECN with trading in the shares of all the top European companies under the name Virt-X (www.virtx.com).

The SSE. As already discussed, the SSE is wholly owned by OM Gruppen. OM Gruppen is listed on the SSE.

The Deutsche Börse. In the past decade, the Frankfurt Exchange (FWB) has transformed itself into Europe's fastest-growing exchange. In 1993, the Deutsche Börse AG (DB) was founded. DB runs the FWB and the German Futures Exchange. It is majority owned by the German banks, and the country's seven other regional exchanges collectively hold a minority share of the new entity.

Government ownership

When a B2B exchange is perceived as providing a significant public benefit, the government may be tempted to assert its national interest during the development of such a market within their jurisdiction. For example, if MetalSite or e-STEEL develops as a dominant exchange for the determination of prices of steel products worldwide, the major steel-producing countries in Asia may decide that they should establish competing steel exchanges in their own countries.

Examples from the securities market

There is now universal recognition that securities markets play a crucial role in mobilizing domestic capital, attracting foreign capital, and allocating scarce resources to the most productive uses. This central role within the economy has led governments to seek to control the operations of the stock exchange. Initially this involved an emphasis on the governing body of the exchange, with a requirement for nonbroker or government representation. More recently, governments have sought an ownership interest in the national stock exchange.

A government with an ownership interest in a stock exchange may also grant that exchange a statutory monopoly. This has the advantage of removing competitive threats in that jurisdiction. On the other hand, if the exchange is given a monopoly, it raises concerns that the securities market may not remain competitive, particularly in today's global economy, in which countries are competing to attract a limited supply of foreign capital.

Examples of exchanges with government ownership are

The Taiwan Stock Exchange. This exchange is owned by the government (39%) and brokers, listed companies, and the public (61%). The public-sector shareholdings are freely transferable, and the stock exchange distributes surpluses as dividends.

The Cayman Islands Stock Exchange (www.csx. com.ky). This exchange is 100% owned by the government.

The Channel Islands Stock Exchange (www.cisx.ci). This exchange is also 100% owned by the government.

THE BROKER DILEMMA

New B2B exchanges that are not owned by the brokers in a market and adopt an open membership structure may face the dilemma of whether to include traditional intermediaries and middlemen, such as brokers, in their new market space or exclude them from membership.

If tiers of distributors, resellers, and brokers dominate a traditional market, the Internet offers the opportunity to disintermediate many of them and enable buyers and sellers to transact business directly with each other through the on-line exchange. The exchange may therefore be tempted to refuse to allow such players to be members of the exchange. In the 1970s, a group of enterprising insurance executives decided to set up a fully electronic Risk Exchange, called REX, to enable companies to buy insurance from primary insurers without going through a costly broker (a sort of early B2B version of Geico Direct). Because their main objective was to disintermediate the brokers, they decided to refuse membership to all insurance brokers. You probably haven't heard of REX, because it failed miserably. The insurance brokers had more market power than the founders imagined and were able to direct insurers not to use the system and persuade them to continue using their familiar brokers.

The alternative approach is to embrace the brokers and other middlemen but ensure that the central, on-line market space is designed in a way that does not favor or advantage the brokers.

If the traditional intermediaries have dominated the existing market, it is critical for a proposed B2B exchange in that vertical to co-opt the brokers into the system so that they bring their deal flow and liquidity to the central market space.

For example, CreditTrade, the on-line credit trading exchange, has joined forces with Prebon Yamane, a leading global credit derivatives intermediary. Under the agreement, Prebon Yamane moved its global credit derivatives team and historical default swap database to CreditTrade in return for a substantial equity stake. In all, 13 credit derivatives brokers in London, New York, and Singapore joined CreditTrade's online credit sales desk to form a single global team. The agreement highlights the potential benefits to all market users of combining the personal attention provided by traditional voice brokers with the speed, efficiency, and cost-effectiveness of an Internet B2B exchange.

One way the exchange can accommodate brokers is to design the system so that a broker's posting or orders are visible only to potential buyers or sellers and cannot be seen by competing brokers. This encourages brokers to use the exchange and to benefit from all the advantages of a centralized, on-line market but without having to let their competitors see any of their deal flow.

CHAPTER SUMMARY

- Unlike e-commerce companies, B2B exchanges have multiple user groups: buyers, sellers, brokers, infomediaries, listed issuers, the public, etc.
- An exchange must remain neutral and balance the competing interests of all its users. Providing an open, fair, and transparent market for all users is essential to an exchange's value proposition and enhances the exchange's ability to attract business.
- Exchanges must embrace the concept of membership in addition to ownership.
- Exchanges owned by one user group (such as the NYSE) have problems with anticompetitive practices. Now broker-owned stock exchanges like the NYSE want to go public because of competition from electronic markets like ECNs.
- Exchanges owned by benign investors are for profit and have open membership (for example, PlasticsNet).
- Calls to run an exchange for the public good may lead to government ownership.
- Exchanges must regulate their members' activities.

- Credibility, integrity, and liquidity are essential to the success of exchanges.
- New exchanges may be tempted to exclude intermediaries, but where the traditional intermediaries have dominated the existing market, a proposed B2B exchange in that vertical must co-opt the brokers into the system so that they bring their deal flow and liquidity to the central market space.

CHAPTER 6

Trading Models

The Internet has enabled a number of different trading models for B2B exchanges. Indeed, on-line B2B trading may be the first business model that truly exploits the unique advantages of the Internet. We believe that the centralized market spaces created by B2B exchanges are the killer application that will drive increased use of the Internet by businesses.

Earlier Internet business models tended to replicate in cyberspace the dynamics of the physical world. The ability to buy a fixed-price plane ticket or a book on-line may be attractive because it is convenient, and we get immediate access to a relatively larger universe of similar fixed-price goods on the Internet. But, like the consumer in the bookstore or at the airline counter, the on-line consumer at Amazon.com or Travelocity.com either accepts a fixed price or clicks away.

By exploiting the power of the Internet, a B2B exchange's on-line centralized trading space facilitates the connecting of buyers with sellers and the generation of dynamic pricing. Dynamic pricing establishes market prices.

By bringing together all the potential buy and sell orders at any particular time and letting those competing offers set the highest price or the price that maximizes the amount sold, the exchange's price can truly be called the market price at that particular point in time. **Dynamic pricing through competitive bidding and auction systems is one of the most exciting features of B2B exchanges and is a key component of the revolutionary nature of B2B Internet commerce.**

THE FOUR NEW TRADING METHODS

As we saw in Chapter 3, the Internet has spawned five new business models for on-line exchanges. These five business models encompass the following four trading methods:

- Fixed pricing (for example, catalog aggregators);
- One-on-one negotiation;
- Auction markets:
  - seller driven;
  - buyer driven (or reverse);
- Electronic autoexecution systems (two-way auctions).

A good B2B exchange will also facilitate the listing of goods or services for sale, the exchange of information, the ability of members to negotiate with each other on price and other features and, eventually, to execute a transaction on-line. The Internet also allows buyers and sellers to trade directly, bypassing traditional intermediaries, which can lower the costs for both parties. A B2B exchange's trading space is global in reach, offers significant convenience, and facilitates a sense of community by fostering direct buyer and seller communication.

BUSINESS MODEL	TRADING METHOD
Aggregators	Fixed prices. Moving toward auctions.
Trading hubs	Fixed prices and some buyer-driven (reverse) auctions.
Post and browse	Individual deals. One-on-one negotiated terms and prices; called the "over-the-counter" market in the securities industry.
Auction markets	Dynamic pricing. Seller-driven and buyer-driven (reverse) auctions.
Fully automated exchanges	Dynamic pricing. Automated matching of orders, continuous auction markets.

Fixed prices: Catalog aggregators

Catalog aggregators aim to provide a one-stop procurement venue for companies. The aggregator streamlines purchasing by aggregating the product catalogs of many suppliers in one place—a web site—and in one format. The parts and products displayed at such a site can number in the hundreds of thousands.

Instead of phoning and faxing multiple potential suppliers, a procurement manager can obtain all the product and pricing information he or she needs in one central site.

EXAMPLES
BigMachines,
e-Chemicals,
PlasticsNet, many
of VerticalNet's
trading hubs

Only a neutral, independent site that is operated by a third party is able to bring many competing sellers together in this way and assure buyers that the information on the site is reliable.

This model works best for the sale of low-priced items that are bought frequently but in small quantities. Accordingly, it does not make sense to negotiate the price on every trade. The prices of products at a catalog aggregator site tend to be static—prices are as stated in the supplier's catalog.

Catalog aggregators can expand their offering by enabling a procurement manager to issue a "request for quotes" to a short list of suppliers through the web site, for large orders or nonstandard items. For example, BigMachines.com aggregates multiple suppliers of industrial machines. Many of these products are custom engineered for the buying client and thus require a tailored selection and configuration technology to enable online collaboration. After machinery selection and configuration, buyers can place a request for quotes and create purchase orders for new engineered machinery directly through BigMachines.com. The BigMachines.com system dynamically generates a machine's unique bill of materials.

e-Chemicals has enhanced its basic system through a joint venture with Yellow Freight that handles the logistics of delivering products to buyers. e-Chemicals takes delivery of the products from the supplier and forwards them to the buyer. Yellow Freight's services enable the buyer to check the order status on-line.

One-on-one negotiations: Post and browse

The most basic form of active trading is the post and browse. This is primarily a structured, and in many cases sophisticated, bulletin board on the web where authorized members of the exchange post expressions of interest to buy or sell or exchange goods or services. In this model, the price in each transaction is negotiated one-on-one.

EXAMPLES
Catex, CreditTrade, PaperExchange

This model is essentially similar to an Internet-based meeting room, but because the exchange prequalifies users before they are authorized to post or to respond to postings on the bulletin board, it is really a private members' room into which only certain types of people are allowed.

Just like a private members' room, the post and browse function creates a virtual community—a group of people who are interested in buying or selling a particular product and can make a connection through the bulletin board.

Most post and browse systems provide a main screen that lists members' postings by one or more categories (for example, by product category or date of posting) and assigns each posting a unique number.

Catex is based on a post and browse model. In the insurance industry, each contract is individually negotiated on the basis of the unique risk features of the properties, goods, or financial exposures that are being insured. It is therefore difficult to prepare standard contracts that can be traded automatically. Instead, the parties need to exchange a lot of information about each other (for example, the credit information on the insured and the underwriting history of the insurer, together with details about the risks to be covered). This necessitates B2B negotiations on every contract. The post and browse feature on Catex enables users to post expressions of interest to buy insurance (that is, cede a risk to an insurer) or sell insurance (that is, offer to assume a particular risk). On the basis of the information posted, the users are able to establish a connection and proceed to negotiate a price and insurance contract between themselves.

CreditTrade provides a similar type of post and browse for institutional players who wish to trade credit default swaps. The parties meet anonymously through the post and browse board and then enter into detailed contract negotiations.

PaperExchange enables a buyer to respond to a price posted on the screen by a seller. The buyer can either accept the price offered or post a counterbid. The seller either accepts the counteroffer or posts a revised price for the buyer to accept or counterbid on.

In addition to this basic match-making functionality the exchange must provide other services to attract new users and support existing users of the system. These services include:

- A method (or methods) for members to communicate with each other to respond to a posting or negotiate the terms of a deal, together with a directory of all users and a way to authenticate messages passed through the system.

- Information about the products on offer that helps buyers understand what is being offered for sale and forums where buyers exchange information and pass on recommendations about products.

- Posttrade information on deals done through the exchange that helps buyers and sellers understand what the market price for a particular product or service is at any point in time.

- Document management services to help parties post, send, and receive trade and supporting documents or prepare contractual documents on-line. This feature enables users to cut down on the use of fax machines and courier companies for exchange of documents and can provide a secure service with authentication and an audit trail of the documents that have been exchanged.

- The legal framework within which the members can trade with legal certainty and with complete trust.
- Security and privacy; often these services will be provided with different levels of security or privacy available as required by different users.

Communication between users of the post and browse feature is critical. The most obvious method is to provide e-mail services. This enables the exchange to build up a Rolodex of the important users in the industry.

However, many users of an exchange will want to retain anonymity, at least in the early stages of a negotiation, to avoid showing their hand too early.

B2B exchanges facilitate this in several ways. The first is to provide for anonymous e-mail. For example, Catex advertises that it provides an "A-Mail" function that enables users to exchange e-mail without disclosing who they are. An additional neat feature of Catex's A-Mail is that once users are ready to disclose who they are, they can check a box that provides for such disclosure. If both parties are using aliases, the system will disclose each party's name to the other only if BOTH have checked the box and approve of simultaneous disclosure of identities.

CreditTrade also provides anonymous broker channels that enable a user to make a connection with another user without revealing their identity (until they are both ready to do so). PaperExchange does not reveal the names of a buyer or seller to any party until they have agreed on a price and quantity through the exchange's anonymous bidding system.

Additional communication channels can be provided by collaborative software applications such as NetMeeting from Microsoft, which enables members to work together on a document or view a presentation, while exchanging real-time conversations on-line.

One area in which post and browse exchanges tend not to get involved is settlement and clearing. Because each trade is individually negotiated between members, the exchange usually requires the members to sort out the transfer of payment and delivery of the goods or services between themselves, without the exchange standing in the middle in any way. However, the exchange can add to its value proposition by introducing back-office functions that support invoicing, accounting, and accurate settlement reports. For example, MetalSite and PlasticsNet enable members to plug their back-office systems into the exchange's systems. PaperExchange also offers a "clearing" process and guarantees payments by certain buyers whose creditworthiness has been approved in advance, which is a value-added service.

Post and browse exchanges are relatively easy to implement, which makes them vulnerable to competitors, and they must quickly evolve more sophisticated trading models (such as auctions) if they wish to enhance their value proposition for the members.

Dynamic pricing: Auction markets

The auction format is likely to become increasingly popular for B2B exchanges, since it enhances efficiency while maximizing the return for the buyer or the seller. In addition, an auction market concentrates the liquidity (that is, all the buy and sell orders) into one specific point in time when the auction closes.

> **EXAMPLES**
> FreeMarkets, Shop2gether, Tradeout

The ability of multiple buyers and sellers to collectively set prices for a wide range of goods and services creates a dynamic pricing model and represents a radical departure from the older, fixed-price model of the Industrial Age.

Until the Internet took off, businesses were forced to pay fixed prices for standardized goods because one-on-one negotiation was inefficient for centralized, mass producers. Now, the advent and growth of Internet-based auctions provide the opportunity for a more efficient, more satisfying relationship between buyers and sellers. In an auction, buyers bid no more than they are willing to pay (and have no excuses for overpaying), and sellers who ask too high a price (by posting a high minimum bid) must soon lower it or choose not to sell. Buyers have increased selection, more convenience, and the opportunity to pay less. Sellers have a larger market and the opportunity to charge more.

On-line auctions developed initially in the C2C space as an efficient way to facilitate person-to-person transactions (for example, the sale of antiques or memorabilia between individuals on eBay). Before the Internet, selling a one-of-a-kind, previously owned item could be difficult. Consumers trying to sell unique products were often constrained to small, localized marketplaces in which to locate potential buyers (for example, flea markets, garage sales, and local classifieds). Now companies like eBay offer consumers a way to put their personal items up for sale on a global basis through on-line auctions.

Seller-driven auctions

In a seller-driven auction, the person lists the item or service for sale, and multiple buyers submit upward price bids for it. This format is used by eBay and tends to lead to an increase in the price bid as the

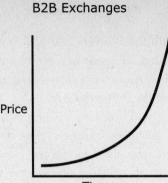

PRICE BIDS IN A SELLER-DRIVEN AUCTION.

close of the auction approaches (see graph). This works well for sellers, who can get the highest price for their goods while using the Internet to maximize their reach to a large number of potential buyers. This facilitates efficient market pricing. Seller-driven auctions work especially well for items that are unique and differentiated but relatively simple to describe and understand.

In the B2B market space, seller-driven auctions are particularly good for liquidating surplus goods. The goods have a well-known first-run market price but are expected to sell at a substantial discount. The auction mechanism replaces the traditional liquidation brokers, who offer only "fire sale" prices. Forrester Research has noticed that as companies use seller-driven auctions more frequently as their standard way of liquidating surplus goods, they are able to move surplus inventory more quickly and thus reduce their overall inventory-holding costs. MetalSite is a good example of a B2B exchange that provides auctions to clear surplus materials for the steel industry.

Seller-driven auctions are less favorable to buyers, because there is no negotiation between the buyer and the seller—just a competition between all the buyers.

Buyer-driven (or reverse) auctions

In buyer-driven auctions, the auction format is inverted, with buyers specifying the items they want and many sellers competing for their business in a downward price auction. This approach clearly favors the buyers, especially if many sellers are offering items that come close to meeting buyers' requirements. In this type of auction, the price tends to fall as the close of the auction approaches (see graph).

The buyer-driven auction is the model adopted by the horizontal trading hubs, such as FreeMarkets and VerticalNet, that facilitate procurement of supplies by companies. The B2B eMarketplace at FreeMarkets operates real-time B2B on-line auctions for companies buying custom industrial-components electronics and commodities such as coal and steel. It uses its auction software to link buyers with sellers in timed reverse auctions in which suppliers place bids to fill an order. FreeMarkets collects fees for conducting the auctions and sometimes takes a percentage of what the buyers save. The company organizes and conducts real-time interactive competitive bidding events that enable large buying organizations (and consortium bids) to purchase industrial materials and components at true market prices. To date, FreeMarkets has executed more than five

PRICE BIDS IN A BUYER-DRIVEN, OR REVERSE, AUCTION.

thousand on-line auctions for more than $7.6 billion worth of goods and services.

The items on which bids are to be placed are grouped into "lots" and then enough suppliers are included to ensure that bidding is competitive. FreeMarkets prevets the suppliers to ascertain that they are acceptable to the buyer and provides the potential suppliers with full details of the items that are being sought (for example, the purchaser's quality requirements). The purchaser is not obliged to accept the lowest bid or to switch from their incumbent supplier. During an on-line auction the suppliers remain anonymous to one another, but they can see competing price bids in real time. The buyer sees both the identity and current bid of each supplier. Auctions typically last one to three hours.

Another good example of this economic model is Shop2gether. Shop2gether enables educational institutions to aggregate their orders for common items such as school furniture and equipment. At a preset time the aggregation of similar orders is closed, and a number of suppliers then bid on that one large collective contract.

The attraction of this format for B2B transactions is that it can substantially reduce a company's procurement costs. However, it works only for items that can be clearly described to the sellers and for which there are plenty of potential suppliers.

Both buyer-and seller-driven auction formats will become increasingly popular, because of the scale, reach, interactive, and real-time attributes afforded by the Internet. We believe that many industries will take advantage of these basic pluses and apply them to B2B exchanges.

One novel application of the reverse auction that we believe is bound to develop is on-line bidding between reinsurance underwriters for property catastrophe programs. As we outlined in our discussion of the post and browse, the wholesale reinsurance industry does not yet have commoditized products—each contract is negotiated individually. In the case of property catastrophe programs, a primary insurer with large property exposures—USAA in Florida, for example—will seek to pass on some of that risk to a reinsurance company, for example XL MidOcean Re in Bermuda. Such property catastrophe reinsurance contracts are negotiated once a year and remain in force until the following year. The present market practice is for the primary insurer to engage a broker (for a large commission), who assists by preparing full details of the property risks to be reinsured. The broker then submits those details (usually by fax and courier mail) to a preselected group of reinsurance underwriters and invites a sealed bid or quotation to be returned by a set date. None of the selected underwriters knows what the other reinsurers have bid, and none of them gets the chance to adjust their bids over the time period.

In the near future, an on-line B2B exchange like Catex, or maybe a horizontal trading hub like FreeMarkets, will offer to run this bidding process as a reverse auction. Underwriters will be able to see the bids made by their competitors on a web site (anonymously, of course) and will be able to adjust their bid downward as the auction time expires.

The result of such competitive bidding on-line is likely to be lower premiums for the primary insurer buying the program and significantly reduced commissions for the broker.

B2B exchanges that offer auction markets are also providing clearing and settlement services. Some sites help the sellers link their back-office systems to the exchange to facilitate real-time inventory checks and fully integrated accounting. The B2B auction exchange should also provide invoicing and credit facilities to encourage businesses to join.

Dynamic pricing: Electronic autoexecution systems

Also emerging quickly are electronic trading systems that automatically match buyers and sellers on a continuous basis and thus create real-time dynamic pricing. **In effect such systems are continuous two-way auctions where the seller offers to sell ("the ask") and the buyer offers to buy ("the bid").** The bid and ask offers must have a fixed (that is, a limit) price or be priced at "market" (that is, at the best price offered on the other side of the market at that precise point in time). The system checks when an order is received to see if it can be immediately matched against an equal but opposite order already in the system. If it cannot be matched, the new order is stored in the system, awaiting arrival of an equal and opposite offer.

Such systems typically give priority to orders that have the best price (the lowest ask and the highest bid) and rank orders with an equal price strictly by time of receipt by the trading engine—a practice called "price-over-time priority." These systems therefore provide a central "limit order book" that allows members to trade on an anonymous, equal, and fair (first come, first served) basis. Automatching systems provide real-time prices and enable fast trading.

Limit order books are effective only if you have

- Standardized or commoditized products that are identical (for example, securities or securitized contracts) or
- High liquidity (lots of competing bid and ask orders flowing into the order book).

If there is little liquidity in the product, it's unlikely that a member's limit order will find an immediate match in the system, and it will sit in the order book until a matching order comes in. For every second that the limit order sits out in the order book, the buyer or seller may be cruelly exposed to changes in the fair market price for the item (because that order can be automatically executed against at any time until he or she cancels it). This makes traders use a "fill or kill" (FOK) approach, whereby they enter an order at a limit price but remove it immediately if it is not instantly matched in the order book. Many electronic trading systems provide a special FOK order type that automatically flushes the order if it does not match.

FOK orders reduce the number of orders in the central order book at any one time and thereby reduce the chances of another order's being matched immediately—a vicious downward spiral that intensifies the lack of liquidity. On the other hand, a liquid market (such as the Nasdaq or NYSE) would be considerably enhanced by a central limit order system, because trades are executed quickly at a low execution cost and with buyers' and sellers' orders being matched directly at the price they offered. In highly liquid and volatile markets it is important to maintain the anonymity of buyers and sellers, since they could significantly affect market prices—so-called market impact—and as we saw in Chapter 2, electronic trading systems are ideally suited for anonymous trading.

Examples from the securities market

Buyers and sellers gathered in a centralized location and operating according to the laws of supply and demand are the key elements of any auction market system for the trading of stocks. Indeed, central limit order book systems have been prevalent in securities markets outside the United States for the last 15 years. The rapid growth of ECNs in the United States in the last two years is due solely to the attractions of a central limit order book system in a highly liquid market. It is interesting to note that the members of Nasdaq have consistently resisted the introduction of a central limit order book on that exchange—perhaps fearing that it would substantially erode the market-makers' profits.

The Bermuda Stock Exchange (BSX) launched a fully automatic trading system in 1998. The BSX system is called Bermuda Electronic Securities Trading (BEST). As a state-of-the-art trading system BEST is a good example of what autoexecution trading systems can offer. It operates as follows:

During the *pretrading period,* orders are entered but are not immediately processed. The purpose of the pretrading period is to allow for price discovery of all existing orders.

Immediately at the start of the *main trading session,* there is an "opening" of the market. At this time, the market determines the opening prices by selecting the price for each security at which the greatest number of shares will trade at the open. If the volume at two different prices would be the same, the system selects the price at which the least volume of unmatched orders will exist. If there is an order imbalance at the opening price, the system automatically allocates the executions based on the time the order was received.

The opening is fully automatic and takes less than a few seconds. Thereafter the market is open for continuous trading until the close of day.

During the main trading session, members enter orders at any time, and the system seeks to match any new orders with the orders already queued in the system on a strict price-over-time priority basis. If an immediate match for a bid or ask order is not available, the order is queued with the best price having priority, and orders with the same price are queued in the order of time of receipt by the trading engine.

Sorting according to price/time priority ensures that bid orders with the highest limit price take precedence over buy orders with lower price limits. Vice versa, an ask order with a lower limit price takes precedence over a sell order with a higher limit price. If there are two equally matched orders, the first order received takes precedence over the other.

There is no *posttrading*. After the market closes, orders are not accepted, processed, or matched. Time-restricted orders are purged from the system, and any "Good Till Cancelled" orders are automatically carried over to the next trading session. The last trade in a security's primary market determines the closing price of a security, whether the trade is made on the same day or before.

BEST supports the creation of multiple markets within the same system and the trading of fixed income and equity securities. The system can operate continuous trading, periodic auctions, and call-over markets. The system supports a variety of order types—market, limit, FOK, and so on. Many features of the system, such as the auction mode, the priority of orders, and the hours of trading, are customizable through a simple parameter-driven administration program.

B2B exchanges with fully electronic trading systems must provide clearing and settlement services to preserve a market's integrity. Since trading is anonymous and executed automatically, it is not practical to have trades being unwound or failing to settle on a regular basis. This means that the exchange has to ensure that settlement happens. In securities markets, this has led to the development of central clearing and depository companies that handle the settlement process and often provide a trade guarantee to trading members.

Successful B2B exchanges will also have to address clearing and settlement issues. In some cases, exchanges may have to take physical delivery of the products sold and handle the logistics of delivering them to the buyer.

ADVANCED NEURAL NETWORKS

More advanced trading systems will inevitably be developed. In the securities area, OptiMark Technologies, Inc. has developed a matching system that enables dealers to express to a secure computer their full trading interest across a continuous range of prices and quantities. The central computers then use patented algorithms to provide a sequential allocation of trades between buyers and sellers at different prices based on a measure of mutual satisfaction. The main advantage of this system is that it enables dealers to achieve more executions without having to expose their full hand to the market, thereby avoiding the hidden costs of market impact.

These patented matching algorithms can be adapted for B2B exchanges to let traders maximize the potential of executing a trade in a periodic auction by allowing them to indicate a range of preferences over a series of parameters on which they seek satisfaction in addition to just price and quantity. In the manufacturing process, for example, quality, time of delivery, and after-sales service can be just as important, and sometimes more important, than price per unit. Similarly, a manufacturer may wish to link a particular purchase, or the amount of that product to be purchased, to another purchase— for example, when both products are needed but in different quantities to manufacture the end product. More sophisticated trading applications are now being developed that allow buyers to build up a profile that indicates their preferences regarding multiple attributes and to link orders for different products into one combination order.

These systems will probably adopt "fuzzy" logic based on neural network technology. Companies like OptiMark, Ariba, Commerce One, and Living-systems.com are currently working on such systems.

LACK OF HUMAN INTERACTION

The buzz on a physical trading floor can sometimes be palpable, especially in the crowd around a trading post where breaking news is creating excitement in a particular product or stock. A common criticism of electronic trading systems, especially from older floor traders in the securities markets, is that computers remove all human interaction from the process.

There are ways to minimize this loss. The first is to add features to the system that are analogs of the physical experience. For example, the trading system can tell you how many other dealers are currently monitoring a particular product or stock at that time, creating the equivalent of the crowd feeling around a particular trading post. Second, an on-line exchange can add around the trading system various community services that increase the level of human interaction between the traders in that market and thus generate the same sense of community that physical floor traders develop (see Chapter 13).

In addition, a B2B exchange should not underestimate the high level of customer support that is required in the early stages to persuade existing corporations to switch the way they do business.

Even after a company joins a B2B exchange, the exchange must provide a full-time trading desk support person who provides human interaction in the form of encouragement to use, and hand-holding in how to use, the exchange's centralized market systems.

THE PANIC BUTTON

All exchanges should provide a mechanism whereby members can withdraw all of their bids and orders from the exchange's system in one go. In BEST, this is a function called "Cancel Orders Globally," which enables the cancellation of all outstanding orders with the click of just one button. This button gives the users absolute assurance that they can get out of the centralized, automated market as quickly as they can put down the phone in their off-line market.

CHAPTER SUMMARY

- Centralized market spaces created by B2B exchanges are the killer application that will drive increased use of the Internet by businesses.

- Trading models for B2B exchanges include catalog aggregators, post and browse, auction markets, and continuous autoexecution systems.

- Catalog aggregators must be neutral, independent sites that are operated by a third party if they are to bring many competing sellers together and earn buyers' trust in the information on the site.

- Just like a private members' room, a post and browse function creates a virtual community—a group of people interested in buying or selling a particular product who can make a connection through a web-based bulletin board.

- Auction sites can provide seller-driven auctions (for example, the auctions run on eBay) or buyer-driven auctions in which suppliers bid competitively for a procurement contract.

- The ability of multiple buyers and sellers to collectively set prices for a wide range of goods and services represents a radical departure from the older, fixed-price model of the Industrial Age.

- Both buyer-and seller-driven auctions will become increasingly popular, because of the scale, reach, interactive, and real-time attributes afforded by the Internet. Many different industries will capitalize on these basic advantages and apply them in B2B exchanges.

- Autoexecution systems work only for identical standardized products (for example, securities or securitized contracts) with high liquidity (lots of competing bid and ask orders flowing into the order book).

- Sophisticated autoexecution systems (like BEST in Bermuda) should support multiple markets, multiple security types, and multiple auction modes and be customizable through parameter-driven administration.
- In the future, trading systems will use "fuzzy" logic to allow traders to input other variables in addition to just price and quantity.
- All exchanges should provide traders with a global trade cancel function—a panic button.

CHAPTER 7

Strategic Partnership Models

As Kevin Kelly points out in his excellent book *New Rules for the New Economy,* the new economy "favors intangible things—ideas, information, and relationships." Forming the right relationships at the startup of a new B2B exchange is critical to the exchange's successful and fast development.

Throughout this book, we emphasize the paramount importance of having industry-specific expertise (vertical knowledge) on board from the start and emphasizing sales, marketing, and customer service. These are the core competencies on which the B2B exchange must focus. All the other ingredients of a good B2B exchange may be obtained through relationships with key strategic partners. In addition, to scale up quickly, B2B exchanges must partner with key suppliers, commerce communities, and information providers.

EIGHT-HUNDRED-POUND GORILLAS AS PARTNERS

In every industry vertical there are eight-hundred-pound gorillas: companies that control the lion's share of the business and are the market leaders. These firms command the respect of the other players in that vertical.

A B2B exchange needs to achieve "buy-in" from one or more of these gorillas if it wants to dominate that vertical and gain enough credibility to persuade the others to follow.

For example, MetalSite was founded and is part owned by three steel mills: LTV Steel Inc. ($4.5 billion), Wierton Steel Corp. ($1.5 billion), and Steel Dynamics Inc. ($450 million). Since then, Bethlehem Steel Corporation and Ryerson Tull, Inc., have joined the exchange in return for equity stakes. Bethlehem Steel is the second largest integrated steel producer in the United States, with shipments of 8.6 million tons a year and annual revenues in excess of $4.4 billion. As sellers, Bethlehem Steel and Ryerson bring significant additional tonnage to the exchange.

Another way to achieve this is for the gorillas to join together to establish the exchange. When this occurs, we call it an industry consortium. Industry consortia raise particular problems, which are analyzed in Chapter 16.

NEUTRALITY ISSUES

Clearly, the introduction of key industry players can affect the perceived neutrality of the exchange, if the "gorilla's hug" is too tight. To counteract any perceived bias, the exchange must develop and maintain a strong, independent advisory board that acts as a counterweight to the purely commercial interests of the industry partners. This is particularly important for an exchange formed by an industry consortium.

MetalSite is now facing competition from e-STEEL, which launched in September 1999. To differentiate itself from MetalSite, the e-STEEL exchange emphasizes its neutrality and independence from the large steel mill owners. e-STEEL's web site, www.e-steel.com, states, "e-STEEL is a true marketplace for the exchange of steel on the Internet. Like other true markets, e-STEEL is neutral, does not own any of the products transacted on the system, and is not affiliated with any industry participant."

Total independence from industry participants is not essential. On the contrary, the buy-in of key industry partners may be critical for success—so long as the exchange is not controlled by such parties and has a strong, independent advisory board (see Chapters 11 and 16).

TECHNOLOGY PARTNERS

Since successful B2B exchanges are fundamentally business solutions, the technology is something that can be outsourced or acquired through a strategic partnership.

e-STEEL is a good example of a successful strategic partnership with a technology expert—Computer Sciences Corporation (CSC). CSC has 49,000 employees in more than seven hundred offices worldwide in areas such as management and information technology consulting, systems consulting and integration, operations support, and information services outsourcing. CSC's revenues exceed $7.4 billion per year.

CSC provided the credibility on the technology side that enabled e-STEEL to quickly build a high level of trust with the main steel-producing companies whose buy-in was critical to the success of the on-line steel exchange.

INFORMATION PROVIDERS

To build value for its members, an exchange must provide as many additional services around the central market space as it can. Rather than building lots of new services, it makes more sense to bring these services in through strategic partners for whom that service is their core competency. This is particularly true in the case of information services.

The classic success story in the information vending business is the meteoric rise of Michael Bloomberg's eponymous company (www.bloomberg.com). Bloomberg started by focusing on the bond trading business. He built up a database of historical pricing information on U.S. bonds that is unrivaled to this day. Around this database he added strong analytic functions to which traders had not previously had instant access. Then he threw in real-time news updates. The Bloomberg box quickly became the only information device that a U.S. bond dealer needed to follow the markets and keep up to date.

Successful B2B exchanges will build into their systems access to tailored information feeds that ensure that a trader in their vertical does not need to go anywhere else for information necessary to trade in that space.

To do this quickly, it makes sense to bring in the information rather than trying to compete with the hundreds of news wire and news syndication services. The Catex risk exchange turned to Hughes Data Services for provision of detailed weather services on their site. MetalSite has formed a partnership with Reuters, who supply customized "Metal Industry" news feeds.

COMMUNITY SERVICES

As we shall see in Chapter 13, a successful B2B exchange must become a virtual community. To do this quickly, the exchange must include a number of value-added community services. The fastest way to do this is to form strategic partnerships with one or more companies that specialize in providing such services. Types of services required, and possible partners, are as follows:

- Customized news feeds (Reuters);
- Documents "extranet" center (IntraLinks);
- Supply chain management (Skyway);
- Escrow services (i-escrow);
- Credit analysis (ecredit.com).

CHAPTER SUMMARY

- To scale up quickly, B2B exchanges must partner with key suppliers, commerce communities, and information providers.
- A B2B exchange needs to achieve buy-in from one or more of the eight-hundred-pound gorillas in its vertical if it wants to dominate that vertical and gain enough credibility to persuade the others to follow.
- Industry involvement must be balanced, however, by a strong and independent advisory board, especially if the exchange is formed by an industry consortium.
- Potential partners include a technology expert.
- Potential partners include information vendors to add real-time news and data services.
- Other partners are providers of additional value services that help build an exchange community.

CHAPTER 8

Revenue Models

Off-line exchanges have established revenue models based largely on the structure of stock exchanges, but the B2B on-line space is creating new forms of revenue opportunities. At present, a B2B exchange can generate almost a dozen types of revenue:

Revenue Source	Stock Exchange Models	Internet B2B Exchanges
Transaction fees	✔	✔
Percentage of cost savings	✘	✔
Posting fees	✘	✔
Subscription (or membership) fees	✔	✔
Listing (or hosting) fees	✔	✔
Information selling fees	✔	✔
Information licensing fees	✔	✔
Advertising and permission marketing fees	✘	✔
Revenue sharing	✘	✔
Software licensing fees	✔	✔
Private networks	✘	✔

TRANSACTION FEES

Since an exchange provides a centralized market space, it follows that if it is successful it can charge a fee for each trade made through it. The usual format is to charge a fee based on the value of the transaction, sometimes with a minimum per trade or a maximum per trade for large deals. On the other hand, transaction fees can discourage trading in the early stages.

Securities exchanges have always charged transaction fees based on the value of the trade. Catex charges a commission on insurance contracts that are concluded as a result of an introduction made in the post and browse at the rate of 10 basis points, or one-tenth of 1%, of the cash value of each transaction. The cost of the commission is borne by the parties involved in the transaction in such proportions as they agree to. At e-STEEL there are no membership or application fees, but e-STEEL charges a transaction fee of 7/8 of 1% to sellers; buyers never pay fees on e-STEEL. Similarly, PaperExchange charges the seller a transaction fee of 3% of the value of the transaction for paper-related and equipment listings. NTE (formerly the National Transportation Exchange) charges a transaction fee based on the size of a load.

With financial services, the value of the security or swap may run into the hundreds of millions of dollars, but the arranging parties are prepared to pay only a very small percentage in transaction fees, or even just a fixed fee. This is due to the enormous amount of competition in that market space, and one of the key issues in securing large mandates is to keep the transaction costs to an absolute minimum.

One issue for a post and browse exchange is how to ensure that the transaction fee is paid, given that members who meet through the bulletin board can easily go off-line to conclude the deal. One solution is for the exchange to have contracts with trading members that require them to report any deals closed as a result of a connection established through the system and then to rely on members' integrity. This can be reinforced in the web site by requiring the parties to communicate through the exchange so that the exchange's administration staff can monitor their activities.

One way to make users communicate through a system in the early stages is to make the initial communications take the form of anonymous postings and responses. This means that the buyer and seller cannot find out each other's identity until after they have exchanged communications within the B2B exchange's system. This way, the exchange can track the deal.

For example, PaperExchange does not reveal the name of the buyer and seller to each other until after they have concluded a trade through the exchange's anonymous bidding system. Similarly, on CreditTrade, the parties to a trade must "lock" the trade in the system once they agree on the terms. The contractual agreement is then finalized off the system, but the parties must come back to the system to either "unlock" the trade, if it did not complete successfully, or confirm that it was executed.

In a relatively small user community this will usually work, since the exchange is likely to hear about trades eventually through industry sources. With an auction system or an electronic execution system, the exchange has a full electronic audit trail for every trade on which to base the transaction fee invoices to members.

One strategic issue for an emerging B2B exchange is whether to forego or reduce the transaction fee in the early stages in order to encourage users to trade through the exchange. Since liquidity is king in persuading industry players to change the way they currently do business and join the exchange, it helps to be able to report significant deal flow through the exchange's facilities. Waiving or reducing the fee at the start for an introductory period helps to bring players onto the exchange and encourages use of the central market space. Charging a transaction fee can also damage the exchange's relationship with key players at the startup stage.

B2B exchanges also have a unique opportunity to charge a buyer based on a percentage of the cost savings that result from the use of the exchange. However, such a fee can be charged only in the year in which the savings actually occur and will decline over time as the size of the savings declines.

POSTING FEE

In lieu of—or in addition to—a transaction fee, an exchange can charge a fee for each "posting," or order entered into the system. For example, in addition to a transaction fee on executed trades, Nasdaq charges a fee for every quote that a market-maker puts into its system.

Again, there is a dilemma of whether to permit free postings initially to encourage volume or whether to charge. One solution to this dilemma is to charge a posting fee but to provide volume discounts that move rapidly toward a zero cost if a player makes a lot of postings (thus adding to the value of the exchange). At PaperExchange, for example, there are no fees for posting bids and offers.

SUBSCRIPTION (OR MEMBERSHIP) FEES

When an exchange registers a new member, it can charge a one-time joining fee and an annual maintenance fee for retaining the membership. This fee can be a lump sum payable in advance each year or a monthly subscription fee for use of the system. Many B2B exchanges waive this fee for a certain period to encourage early membership.

Internet-based exchanges can track this easily by implementing secure user name and password access to the trading screens and other members-only parts of the web site. Clearly, it is attractive to new members if they can sign up for a free trial period or if they can access the site to view information—but not to post offers or respond to offers—for a reduced fee or for no charge. The Credit-Trade web site permits you to register as a "visitor" for free, which provides you with access to parts of the site but not to the crown jewels—the trade postings of potential deals. PaperExchange allows all visitors to see the live postings, but a user name and password are necessary to respond or counterbid. PaperExchange does not currently charge any joining fees.

LISTING (OR HOSTING) FEES

Exchanges that permit users to list products on the system for trading can charge those users a fee for "listing" the products.

In securities exchanges, this has taken the form of a listing fee that is charged whenever an issuer has securities admitted to listing and trading on the exchange. It should be noted that in this case, the exchange assumes a regulatory role with respect to securities listed on the exchange and establishes a direct contractual relationship with issuers of the securities. For example, the exchange ensures that issuers make full disclosure to the market regarding any information that might affect the price of the securities, the volume of trading, or their ability to meet their financial commitments (what stock exchanges call "price-sensitive information"). Some stock exchanges admit securities for trading without listing them, in which case they have no direct relationship with issuers of the securities and do not profess to regulate them. The Bermuda Stock Exchange (BSX), for example, allows trading members to print trades made in securities that are listed on the NYSE or Nasdaq even though those securities are not listed on the BSX.

For B2B exchanges that trade physical products, this fee can take the form of a hosting charge to suppliers for them to set up their virtual storefront within the exchange's web site.

For example, VerticalNet charges a fee to host the supplier's storefront and list the supplier's products in its commerce-enabled web site. These hosting or listing fees currently comprise the majority of VerticalNet's revenue stream.

INFORMATION SELLING FEES

Once an exchange has established the power of its central market, it has the economic power to charge users for valuable information that only the exchange has, such as the trading information for each day and historical trading data.

Securities markets use information vendors to disseminate securities information globally and charge them for receiving their data feeds from the exchange. Reuters, Bloomberg, and Bridge/Telerate are the largest information vendors and they all pay a fee to the larger stock exchanges to receive a real-time feed of trading and pricing data from them. The information available from smaller exchanges is not as valuable to the information vendors, so they generally will not pay a fee for it, but they are usually willing to carry the data on their systems in order to claim that their screens are the most comprehensive information sources.

Some B2B exchanges take the view that the trade data is so valuable that they must restrict access to it to paying subscribers only. In some markets, the trade data available on deals made through the B2B exchange is unique information that was not previously available to players in that market space, and the exchange wants to preserve the value of that information by restricting access to it. For example, Manheim Online charges a fee for car dealers to buy the list of all the sale prices from the on-line auctions held each day. Clearly, the current fair market value of used cars sold through the web site is very valuable information to the dealers.

This approach limits the initial visibility of the exchange and can slow down the overall rate of take-up in the industry. On the Internet it is often sensible to give information away at the start in order to build your market share and develop relationships with users.

New B2B exchanges should build market awareness of their exchange by providing the widest dissemination of their trade information, including making it freely available at the beginning. The exchange can look to charge a fee for the data if they develop to the point where their information is truly unique and valuable.

INFORMATION LICENSING FEES

The pricing information that comes out of an active exchange can sometimes be used to create new products, such as futures or options contracts that are "derived" from the cash prices. Derivative contracts can themselves be traded. In these circumstances, the exchange can charge a licensing fee for the use of the pricing data used in the formulation of the derivative contracts.

In the securities world, the most obvious examples of this are the Dow Jones and Standard & Poor's indices in the United States. Each index is based on the prices at which the constituent stocks trade on the NYSE or Nasdaq. Standard & Poor and Dow Jones charge large license fees to the Chicago Mercantile Exchange and the Chicago Board of Trade, respectively, for the use of those indices to trade derivative contracts. If the NYSE and the Nasdaq had formulated those indices, they would be able to charge a license fee for the use of the data. In the United Kingdom, the London Stock Exchange has a 50/50 joint venture with the *Financial Times* called FTSE International, which creates and publishes the leading equity and bond indices in the United Kingdom and Europe. The FTSE 100 index is based on the pricing data published by the London Stock Exchange.

ADVERTISING AND PERMISSION MARKETING FEES

In the Internet Age, a B2B exchange that establishes itself as a portal in a specific industry vertical can charge fees for banner advertising and other extended listing services on its web site.

VerticalNet is a good example of a B2B exchange that already derives a substantial part of its revenue from advertising, or sponsorships, carried on its web site.

Extended listings are similar to on-line Yellow Pages. The B2B exchange provides a comprehensive directory of the key industry players or a collection of suppliers' storefronts and charges firms a premium price to enlarge or enhance their listing with graphics, hypertext links to their own web sites, and so on.

Advertising on the web is evolving rapidly. Many people have already realized that banner ads are not effective on the web and, in fact, have been poorly received. The good news is that when it comes to Internet advertising, banners are not the only game in town. "Opt-in" e-mail marketing—sending commercial e-mail messages to targeted lists of Internet users who have opted in to receive them—is generating click-through rates as high as 20% and helping publishers, catalogers, and e-commerce companies reach their target markets quickly, cheaply and responsibly.

Customer retention and loyalty are two key themes that B2B exchanges must use to differentiate themselves from the competition. All registered users of the exchange can be opt-in recipients of information in areas of interest that they have indicated on sign-up. Members should therefore be offered the choice of opting in to certain targeted e-mail advertisements when they subscribe to the exchange—perhaps for a reduced subscription fee. In this way, the B2B exchange can participate in the rapidly growing market for opt-in e-mail marketing—now called "permission marketing"—by carefully selling access to its membership list.

REVENUE SHARING FEES

B2B exchanges can generate revenues through strategic partnerships with business partners who provide analytics, ratings, and news services or can publish and sell their own data and analytics.

Stock exchanges have traditionally missed the opportunity to provide information and analytical services around the central market trading facility. This is because the stock exchanges have been owned by the brokerage firms, who themselves make a lot of money from providing such information and analytical research to their investment clients. To avoid competing with their owners, stock exchanges generally have not used the information generated by their own exchange; instead they have allowed their broker members to use that data.

New B2B exchanges that are structured as for-profit, open-membership exchanges must take full advantage of the opportunities to generate revenue from advanced analytical research and data reporting services. Although the exchange cannot provide direct recommendations on the products available for trading on the exchange, it can sell all of the raw data and analytical services that are required for buyers and sellers to make informed trading decisions.

SOFTWARE LICENSING FEES

If the exchange develops a sophisticated trading platform with integrated logistics and back-office functionality, it may license this software to other exchanges in different verticals that are not directly competitive.

However, a number of software companies, such as Ariba, CommerceOne, Maoi Technologies, RightWorks, and i2 Technologies, are now specializing in producing trading system software for multiple B2B exchanges. It makes more sense to partner with one of these specialist suppliers than to spend a lot of time developing software with a view to licensing it to other exchanges. Indeed, stock exchanges have traditionally developed their own internal systems at huge expense and then found that outside software specialists develop more efficient systems that get licensed to competing exchanges.

PRIVATE NETWORKS

As an exchange grows, it can create private markets for large buyers or direct buyer-supplier connections, leveraging its core trading technologies. The development of a private network enables an exchange to charge a monthly administration fee, which is more dependable revenue than transaction fees. Exchanges such as BigMachines, Catex, and CreditTrade are setting up and operating private networks for their members.

Catex advertises that they can assist in the development of a customized Internet-based distribution network for individual subscribers. The core system is "whitelabeled" for the client: All references to Catex and the Catex subscriber community are removed, so that the private network owner creates their own Internet business solution to communicate with their business partners and clients. For example, a number of Catex subscribers have commissioned the exchange to develop a version similar to the Catex core software to allow them to receive facultative submissions via the Internet. These private networks can then be tied into the B2B exchange's core system and are a good way to forge strategic relationships with key industry participants.

CHAPTER SUMMARY

- New exchanges need to waive the transaction fee or provide discounts for volume trades in the early stages.
- Posting fees may discourage early use of the site.
- To attract liquidity, an exchange may need to give discounts for volume of postings/transactions.
- Listing fees and product introduction fees include charging suppliers a fee to host their virtual storefronts at the exchange.
- Membership fees (initial and annual) may create potential conflict between driving early membership and raising revenue.
- The sale of data and other services (for example, stock exchanges sell price, volume, and transaction data) may create a conflict between opening access to information and raising revenue.
- New B2B exchanges should build market awareness of their exchange by providing the widest dissemination of their trade information, including making it freely available at the beginning.

Exchanges can charge a fee for the data if they develop to the point where their information is truly unique and valuable.

- Advertising (sponsorship) and permission marketing fees are unique to the Internet and can be a part of a B2B exchange's revenue.

- B2B exchanges should seek revenue-sharing models with analytics, ratings, and news services.

- Software licensing fees are wonderful if you can get them, but exchanges should let specialist software companies develop and license the systems.

- Running private networks is a good way to generate regular revenue and forge strategic relationships with key industry participants.

Part III

SEVEN SECRETS FOR SUCCESS FOR B2B EXCHANGES

CHAPTER 9

Secret 1: Stay Focused— Specialize in a Vertical

The most important secret to success in the initial phases of developing a B2B exchange is to target a specific industry in which you have strong expertise and then *specialize in a vertical* within that industry.

Specialization enables you to dominate your chosen space quickly, which creates mind share and liquidity, and then helps you to scale up quickly. Specialization also lets you tailor your business model to match the target market's distinct characteristics. These are critical success factors at the start.

Once your exchange has dominated your chosen vertical, you can widen your scope into other verticals within your chosen industry, but you can achieve this luxury only if you have proven liquidity and have demonstrated your ability to dominate.

An exchange's main value proposition is in bringing together and matching up buyers and sellers; it follows therefore that a successful exchange brings together buyers and sellers who are interested in buying or selling the same, or similar, products. In the physical world, a car auction is not followed by a cattle auction, because each of these markets has different players and requires different storage and delivery mechanisms. In the virtual world, the differences between on-line markets may not be as pronounced, but they still exist and the players in each market are very different. Hence the need to specialize at the start.

MetalSite (www.metalsite.net) is a good example of an exchange that had a specific focus from the outset. Situated as a trading hub for the steel industry, MetalSite started off trading surplus or second-grade metals only. This unique specialization allowed it to dominate that vertical. They selected these products initially because the existing players felt they could participate in a new market for those products without threatening their core businesses. Having established a good name, some great publicity, and a proven ability to trade substandard steel, MetalSite is now able to expand its product range and to introduce primary-grade steel as a product.

Not every exchange will be a winner in its chosen vertical space; only the sites with proven liquidity will succeed. **In the exchange business, liquidity is king. Sellers gravitate to the market that has the most buyers, and buyers like the market that has the best supply.**

Once you start to dominate a particular market, you can quickly build further market share, because your proven liquidity attracts more suppliers and thus more buyers—in a virtuous spiral.

VERTICAL PORTALS

Industry sectors can be divided into "vertical" market spaces, or divisions due to geography, regulations, or product characteristics. These divisions act like fissures in the on-line world and allow different B2B exchange markets to service different verticals.

Regulatory Division. In the securities markets a regulatory division is evident between securities that are registered with the U.S. Securities and Exchange Commission (SEC) and therefore can be sold to the U.S. public and securities that are not registered in the United States. The Bermuda Stock Exchange (www.bsx.com), which is not subject to regulation by the SEC, is able to develop as a unique stock exchange by specializing in securities not registered in the United States, even though it is located less than 780 miles from the NYSE.

Product Division. An example of product differentiation is MetalSite's initial specialization in scrap metals rather than primary-grade steel. The industry is the same, the steel industry, but the product differentiation has enabled MetalSite to build a dominant position in those products.

In other words, a laserlike focus on a specific product category, or vertical within an industry, can still yield a profitable space for a unique B2B exchange.

Geographical Division. A good example of a market divided by geography is the market for electricity. Electricity is a difficult product, because it has to be consumed quickly after it is generated (you cannot store megawatts of power on a warehouse shelf) and it cannot be transported too far from the generator. This means that power generated in the United States cannot be exported to an overseas market, such as Europe.

As a result, the vertical spaces available for B2B exchanges in the electricity market are divided by geographical location.

This has enabled a successful B2B electricity market to develop in Scandinavia (www.skm.se), at the same time as HoustonStreet.com and Altra Energy have developed as separate B2B electricity exchanges in the United States. When a product can be shipped around the world, the vertical market space for that product is global and the dominant B2B exchange is likely to be a global market, unless there are regulatory barriers that prevent a truly global market from developing.

Diagonal Divisions. Another special type of market space is where the buyers and sellers are sufficiently homogenous in their interests that they represent a unique "vertical," even though they cut across several industries. For example, small business buyers can have identical interests in aggregating their orders for many types of product in order to secure better prices. Similarly, the sellers of excess inventory and surplus goods are sufficiently homogenous across multiple industries to support a specific vertical focus. This is the space that Tradeout is targeting. A special market space that cuts across multiple horizontal markets can be called a "diagonal."

CHOOSE A MONSTER MARKET

The size of some of these B2B markets is enormous. For example, in the United States the market for paper is worth at least $650 billion (PaperExchange), the market for steel is $600 billion (MetalSite and e-STEEL), and the market for plastics is $390 billion per annum. Worldwide, the market for wholesale reinsurance (excluding life products) is at least $100 billion in premiums (Catex), and the machinery industry is a $1 trillion market (BigMachines).

Some markets are more active than others. For example, the market for nuclear power stations is worth several billion dollars, but they are bought and sold infrequently. Conversely, in the paper industry there are lots of trades each day.

It obviously makes more sense to focus on the monster markets, where there is frequent trading and the most profits will be made.

VERTICAL KNOWLEDGE

Experienced vertical industry professionals should develop B2B exchanges. With entrepreneurial exchanges, the founders should be working within their chosen industry but should have the vision to see that with Internet technologies now being adopted by business, there is an enormous opportunity to leave the Industrial Age corporations and start up a B2B exchange. These professionals have deep knowledge of their particular industry and strong relationships with the main buyers and sellers in that vertical space. Alternatively, an exchange could be founded by a group of existing players within an industry and spun off as an independent, neutral entity.

Vertical knowledge is critical for the exchange to build credibility within the vertical quickly and ensure that it is customized for that particular market.

The vertical knowledge of the founders of an exchange can be a major barrier to entry for potential competitors. Accordingly, a startup B2B exchange should concentrate on the vertical in which its founders have the most industry experience or in which it can most easily buy in that expertise.

CASE STUDY: THE EFFECTS OF GLOBALIZATION ON SECURITIES MARKETS

The recent success of electronic communication networks (ECNs) in attracting market share away from the traditional stock exchanges is a timely warning for all traditional markets: The Internet is globalizing markets that were previously constrained by geography.

During the first half of the twentieth century, stock markets flourished in all of the free-market developed economies. Local stock exchanges proliferated—for example, there used to be 13 stock exchanges in the United Kingdom, and there are still 21 regional stock exchanges in India. Local markets could exist because the securities were evidenced by physical stock certificates (which had to be physically delivered to the buyer to effect settlement), and because the companies traded on these regional exchanges were mainly small companies with a local flavor. As the trading world expanded and companies became first national and then international, their shares were traded on a more national and then international basis. This led to pressure on the local exchanges to merge into one national exchange to pool the liquidity in these securities. In 1976, for example, the London Stock Exchange absorbed the 13 regional exchanges into one national stock exchange. Now the growth of international investment flows is generating pressure to create global exchanges.

The next major innovation was the development of central securities depositories (CSDs). A CSD immobilizes the physical certificates, which represent stocks and bonds, and creates instead book-entry records of ownership. The result is that share trades can be settled electronically without any transfer of physical paper. Now shares can be traded electronically in a continuous, auction market system (see Chapter 5) and then settled electronically. This enables massive volumes to be traded—for example, on a good day in New York in 2000 more than 1 billion shares changed hands—and for investors' orders to be received from all over the world.

Today, the world's largest stock exchanges are in turmoil. The acceptance of the Internet as one global communications standard has enabled electronic trading systems, called ECNs in the United States, to develop a global reach in less than three years; whereas it took the NYSE more than two hundred years to build its global reach and brand name. Suddenly the anticompetitive restrictions and cost inefficiencies that have developed within the broker-owned and -controlled traditional stock markets are being cruelly exposed.

ECNs are for-profit entities and fully electronic, so they are driving down the cost of trading and are providing pricing efficiencies by using central limit order books to directly match buy and sell orders.

The only way forward for older exchanges is to demutualize and become more competitive. This is evidenced by the headlong rush of the NYSE, Nasdaq, and London and Toronto Stock Exchanges to announce that they are turning themselves into for-profit shareholder companies and going public themselves. However, not all of the brokers who own these securities exchanges will agree to upset the status quo and reshape their profitable ways of doing business. For example, the members of the International Petroleum Exchange—a derivatives market based in London—rejected the management's proposals to demutualize.

The small traders and local members who own and control the world's largest derivatives markets in the world—the Chicago Board of Trade (CBOT) and the Chicago Mercantile Exchange (CME)—are facing the same tsunami. Both exchanges have long defended their open outcry pit trading, despite the enormous cost of bringing thousands of traders together on huge trading floors, and have restricted the voting power of the large institutional firms who provide the capital that supports their markets. Indeed, the very existence of two competing derivatives markets the size of the CBOT and CME in the same city—each with its own clearinghouse and billion-dollar trading floor—is testimony to some of the inefficiencies of the Industrial Age. **In the new economy, the winner takes most, and successful B2B exchanges will so effectively dominate their chosen verticals that two similar exchanges will not be able**

to coexist for as long as the Board of Trade and the "Merc" (as they are affectionately called) have.

On an electronic platform it is possible to trade all forms of securities, including stocks, bonds, and derivatives, side by side. This fact has undermined the previous physical separation of stock exchanges (the NYSE and Nasdaq) from commodities exchanges (the CBOT and CME). As a result, securities markets outside the United States have been rapidly consolidating the trading of shares and derivatives into one exchange. In Germany, the Deutsche Börse now operates both markets. In Amsterdam, the oldest stock exchange in the world and the European Options Exchange derivatives market have merged to form Amsterdam Exchanges. In Sweden the OM Gruppen now owns and operates the stock exchange and the derivatives market. In Hong Kong and Singapore, the respective governments mandated the merger of the stock and derivatives exchanges.

The race is now on to create one global market space for all types of major financial securities, including shares, bonds, and derivatives, and in the end, there is likely to be only one big winner.

Nasdaq has recently merged with the American Stock Exchange (AMEX), which, interestingly enough, already trades options contracts and holds a license to run a futures market in the United States, and has announced deals to link up with exchanges in Japan, Australia, and Hong Kong and possibly the Deutsche Börse in Europe. Meanwhile, the Deutsche Börse and London Stock Exchange would each like to establish a pan-European electronic exchange for the top three hundred securities in Europe.

However, this global market space will only exist for a small percentage of securities—those that can command worldwide liquidity and attention. This is why the proposed pan-European exchange is focusing on the top 300 securities only. There will still be a role for national stock exchanges in trading the securities of companies that do not have global appeal and acting as nurseries for small, high-growth companies that have the aspiration to one day be traded on what we call the "Global 1,000" system. But, in the future, purely national exchanges will have to face the reality of seeing their biggest and best stocks moving on to the global market space.

In the same way, other markets will be divided into global market spaces; purely national market spaces; and small local market spaces.

We have analyzed this globalization effect in some detail because it will effect all businesses that operate outside of a purely local context. The securities markets have been affected so rapidly and noticeably because they were already relatively efficient and trade products that are now totally digital, fungible and fully commoditized.

In the next ten years, most physical markets will be affected by the same dynamics and face the same global competitive pressures. They will witness the walls of their ancient citadels shake and then crumble.

Blowing their trumpets at the ramparts will be the B2B exchanges that are now emerging.

THE RAINFOREST EFFECT

In the ecosystem of a rainforest, there is intense competition among the vegetation to reach the sunlight. Covered by the dense canopy of the overhanging trees, many plants learn to live in the shadows and provide ground cover. Others thirst for greater glory and have to grow thin, tall, and fast in order to pierce through the existing canopy and break out into the sunlight above. Once those high achievers reach the light, they can afford to spread out, develop branches and leaves, and add to the lush green canopy.

In the same way, B2B exchanges must focus on a vertical, scale up quickly, and grow as fast as they can. Once they break through the canopy and achieve dominance, mind share, and credibility in that vertical, they can afford to spread out and introduce new products, attack other verticals, and add extra services.

For example, PaperExchange started off in the containerboard and fine-paper segments. Once it had dominated these product verticals, it incorporated all major grades of paper, including paperboard, newsprint, and scrap paper products. Now its web site includes listings of equipment and machinery, from presses and corrugators to an entire mill, for sale.

PaperExchange's potential rivals are now facing the sunlight starvation of plants that are growing underneath the forest canopy.

CHAPTER SUMMARY

- Target a specific industry.
- An industry may be fissured by geography, regulations, or product characteristics—select a vertical within an industry and specialize in it.
- Specialization helps you scale up quickly and dominate your space.
- Successful exchanges tailor their business model to match their target market's distinct characteristics.
- The striking effects of globalization on stock exchanges provide a lesson for all markets in the next 10 years—but global trading will be relevant only to a very small group of securities, leaving opportunities for smaller national exchanges.
- Once you have dominated one vertical, you can expand your product range based on your credibility and perceived expertise (the rainforest effect).

CHAPTER 10

Secret 2: Play to Win— The Need to Dominate

The benefits of specialization, which we describe in Chapter 9, mean that there will be only one major winner in each vertical sector. That winner will take the most in the vertical. Consequently, a successful exchange must try to be one of the "first to market" in its chosen vertical.

This powerful new paradigm derives from the fact that on an electronic Network, success is self-reinforcing and driven by the dynamics of increasing returns. Increasing returns will lead to a concentration of buyers and sellers in one B2B exchange market space for each product. One B2B exchange may operate several market spaces, but only one centralized market space is likely to dominate for each product.

In true pioneering fashion, the founders of a new B2B exchange on the Internet must plant their flag, declare victory, and then run like hell.

VIRAL GROWTH

With respect to B2B exchanges, the law of increasing returns means that the site with the most or the best buyers will attract the most or the best suppliers, which will generate transaction liquidity, which will attract more buyers. **Liquidity attracts more liquidity in the exchange business.**

Once this virtuous circle has been set in motion, it turns into a vortex, sucking more players into the exchange and becoming self-sustaining in a virtual perpetual motion.

In addition, this virtuous vortex creates a "positive polarity" that repels potential competitors. Since the successful exchange is generating the most liquidity and attracting the key players in that vertical

1. This attracts key players (big buyers)
2. This attracts more buyers

This creates a virtual community

1. This attracts the key sellers (big suppliers)
2. This attracts more sellers

This generates liquidity in the form of transactions

THE VIRTUOUS VORTEX.

market space, it becomes difficult for a competitor to get enough traction to start such a virtuous circle in its favor. One of the main reasons for this is that players who join a successful exchange are reluctant to move to another exchange. A key player is unlikely to switch easily to another startup exchange once it has

- Gone through the sign-up process with one exchange;
- Got used to trading through that exchange; and
- (If the exchange follows Secret 7 in the formula for success we present in this book) integrated its back-office systems and document processing with that exchange.

This means that a successful exchange that starts to dominate a vertical market space can create very high barriers to entry in that space.

Clearly, the first credible exchange to market has a significant advantage in establishing its name and approaching the key players before any other exchange. However, in the more traditional industries, being the first exchange may not always mean being the winner, since it may take a long time to build up industry acceptance of this new business model. In such situations, the second or third mover may be able to learn from the mistakes of the first and benefit from the groundwork established by the first mover in selling the concept of an exchange mechanism. In addition, if the second mover has greater industry-specific experience (vertical knowledge) and greater credibility, it can gain more market acceptance and become the dominant player.

LIQUIDITY, LIQUIDITY, LIQUIDITY

Achieving domination means having the greatest liquidity, that is, having the most trades done on your exchange. The main service an exchange provides is a centralized market space, and the more likely a buyer or seller is to make a satisfactory transaction on your exchange, the more likely they are to sign up and use your exchange over its rivals.

Because liquidity is king for exchanges, it is essential to build trading volume as quickly as possible.

Building the volume of trades is more important than increasing the number of members at the start. Target the key players who are likely to trade the most and get them to join early, rather than focusing on signing up the most members. In addition, if there are any intermediaries who can "make a market," they are like gold dust at the start. They'll help you create liquidity by smoothing out natural timing fluctuations in the number of buyers or sellers who are available at any particular point in time.

In the securities business, liquidity has always been king. Nasdaq has succeeded as a market for smaller company stocks (which are naturally illiquid) by providing two market-makers for each stock. These market-makers quote a bid and an ask price for their designated stocks on a continuous basis. The result is that investors can always trade in those stocks (albeit at the additional cost of paying the market-makers' "spread," as discussed in Chapter 6). The success of the London Stock Exchange in the 1980s was built on the fact that it provided a more liquid market for trading many European stocks than did the domestic market for those shares. For example, more Swedish companies' shares were trading in London than on the Stockholm Stock Exchange, and about one-fifth of German shares were trading there rather than on the many regional exchanges in Germany. In fact, London became such a dominant market for trading European shares that the London Stock Exchange changed its name to the International Stock Exchange. This domination arose because London had a critical mass of large securities houses, many of whom were prepared to make a market in these European securities from their dealing desks in London.

Interestingly, both the Stockholm Stock Exchange and the Deutsche Börse have managed to reengineer themselves and win back a dominant position in Swedish and German securities, respectively, by

- Abandoning the broker-owned model of ownership and closed membership through demutualization (see Chapter 5);
- Turning themselves into profit-focused, commercial operations;
- Adopting electronic trading systems that provide more efficient trading than London's market-maker system;
- Merging with rivals and competing regional exchanges to achieve dominance.

The International Stock Exchange in London, on the other hand, failed to modernize during the early 1990s. Now it has lost its dominant position in most European securities and has changed its name back to the London Stock Exchange. Today, all the traditional stock exchanges in Europe face fresh competition from the new B2B exchanges called electronic communications networks, such as POSIT, Tradepoint, Easdaq (which has just been restructured as a pan-European platform for low-cost securities trading), Jiway, and a proposed new institutional crossing network called CrossNet.

CRITICAL MASS OF USERS

Liquidity is enhanced if you can build a critical mass of users as quickly as possible. To do this you must target the key players in your vertical, be they buyers or sellers, and make sure they sign up with you. To achieve sign-up, most exchanges have to waive the standard subscription fees in the early stages, even though waiving fees at the start can put a lot of pressure on an exchange's finances.

Market share is worth more than profits in the early stages of a B2B exchange.

In the B2C world, we have seen the development of a new valuation model, which is based not on current net income but on future revenue potential, in order to capture the dynamics of the new economy. The same dynamic of increasing returns applies to B2B exchanges, so achieving domination in the early years can ensure future revenues in that vertical.

Signing up key players also creates a forward momentum that captures mind share as press releases and the standard "jungle telegraph" within each vertical pass on the word about the growth of an exchange. Conversely, a low growth rate in the early stages can result in a serious loss of credibility. If an exchange creates significant awareness at the launch and then does not deliver a credible level of transactions within a reasonably short time, it will be harder to sign up more members.

A successful exchange organizes a massive marketing and customer care program to win converts quickly. New users must be wooed, cajoled, and encouraged to sign up early and then smothered with good customer support to ensure that they use the exchange. This includes providing free training for each member's staff and constant contact with the member to make sure that indifference does not prevent them from trading on your exchange in the early stages. For example, e-Chemicals places ads focused on customer acquisition in chemical trade publications. The company's retention marketing efforts include follow-up communications via e-mail for new customers who have subscribed to the site, as well as direct mail pieces and auction invitations. e-Chemicals has a dedicated, direct sales force to sell its e-commerce procurement to large customers and suppliers and targets small customers through telemarketing and direct marketing efforts.

One choice to make early on is whether to target buyers or sellers initially. An exchange must attract both, but initially it is critical to attract a sufficient number of the party who will gain more from transacting over an exchange than they would from traditional transaction mechanisms. In the new economy, this is likely to be the buyers, since they are usually empowered more by the introduction of Internet-based automation of the trading process. However, this is not always the case. For example, both PaperExchange and MetalSite have succeeded by targeting sellers first.

MetalSite initially secured commitments from major steel producers to list inventory on a daily basis and a substantial volume of product for sale monthly. These steel suppliers were leaders and innovators in the national and international marketplaces and brought both credibility and product to MetalSite. Sometimes it takes market-makers to get a market going. For example, because electricity is not a commodity that sticks around, it is important to have both buyers and sellers participating at the same time. To guarantee market liquidity and ensure that deals can always be closed, HoustonStreet has made a deal with Enron Online to ensure that Enron's buy and sell quotes are always available on HoustonStreet.com.

Once a winner has critical mass, there are very high barriers to entry for other potential exchange competitors, since inertia prevents members from shifting from one exchange to another.

DOMINATION VERSUS ANTIDILUTION

To achieve market domination in a chosen vertical when building a B2B exchange, look to merge with competitors to gain a dominant position as quickly as possible. e-STEEL is some six months behind MetalSite in the steel industry vertical. The huge chemicals market now has several competitors, including CheMatch, SqiQuest, e-Chemicals, and Chemconnect. In this scenario, one exchange is likely to gain a dominant position and suck the oxygen out of the others. For the exchanges that find themselves in second or third place, there is no point worrying about trying to maintain market share against each other; they must merge and seek domination.

Winning as a B2B exchange is about dominating your vertical; it is not about coming in second or third while trying to avoid dilution of your existing market share.

For example, in September 1999, PaperExchange, the world's leading Internet trading marketplace for the pulp and paper industry, announced the acquisition of MPX, Inc., the developer of Mpexchange, an Internet-based, third-party exchange for white paper grades. The acquisition expanded PaperExchange.com's already strong user base and strengthened its domination in printing and writing grades. For the founders of Mpexchange, the chance to join with Paper-Exchange and dominate the market was far more attractive than competing with them for market share.

Cash Cappel, CEO of MPX, Inc., is quoted in the company's September 1999 press release as stating, "We had been moving aggressively towards the launch of Mpexchange later this month; however, the opportunity to join forces with PaperExchange.com, the pioneer and by far the strongest on-line paper-based trading environment, was an incredible opportunity and too compelling to pass up. We are delighted to join forces with the very talented and focused PaperExchange team and contribute to increasing their market dominance."

On the other hand, don't forget that industries can be fragmented along many lines, geographical, regulatory, or product category–related. This means that several exchanges may coexist in the same industry. Having complementary exchanges in the same industry can actually help build an exchange by increasing awareness and acceptance of exchanges in that industry at the early stage. Subsequent mergers can ensure that an exchange dominates the whole industry sector.

BRANDING

Building a strong brand name is very helpful in achieving domination. The NYSE brand is powerful in the securities industry in the United States and abroad, and Nasdaq struggles to compete with the pull of the "Big Board." In the paper industry, PaperExchange has already established a strong brand, and in the U.S. transportation business, NTE (formerly the National Transportation Exchange) already has strong branding.

One element of branding is the name. In many cases this is determined by what Internet domain names are still available, so make sure you first check what is available. It helps if the name is short, catchy, and—above all else—pronounceable. Moai is an example of a strange-sounding word (it's pronounced Mow-Eye). On its web site, the company has to explain that it took its name from the giant stone statutes found on Easter Island and chose it because the statues "instill in us a deep sense of wonder, and they remind us to think big and wild—to dare to do the impossible."

One danger in choosing a name is being too product specific at the start. Initially this may help in building brand recognition in your chosen vertical, but later it can become constraining as you expand the exchange into other complementary verticals and outgrow the name. For example, PaperExchange is very product specific. The alternative is to choose a more general catchy name, like Tradeout.com.

The Catastrophe Risk Exchange has established a strong brand name, "Catex," in the insurance industry. Initially their focus was on trading high-value property catastrophe risk contracts (known as "cat" contracts in the business). However, the name Catex could now be seen as a hindrance, because it requires the exchange to constantly explain that they are NOT limited to catastrophic risk products. CEO Frank Fortunato is quoted in an *Insurance Networking* article as saying that "a common misconception is that Catex focuses solely on catastrophe exposures. . . . but Catex actually facilitates various risks, including environmental liability, marine, aviation, auto insurance and others; less than 50% of transactions involve catastrophe exposures." On the other hand, the Catex name is now widely recognized in the industry and a change would require a significant rebranding.

The same problem has been highlighted in the B2C world, where companies such as eToys and Software.net have found that their name does not suit them as they grow. Software.net expanded from just software into game cartridges and some hardware products, so it decided to change its name to Beyond.com. On the other hand, a generic name like "Amazon.com" continues to work even though the company has expanded from simply book selling to on-line auctions, music and video, and other sales.

One option is to make up a name. The industry consortia for the auto industry has abandoned the descriptive brand "autoexchange" for the made-up name Covisint (pronounced KO-vis-int). Apparently the name is a combination of "connectivity, collaboration and communication," "visibility and vision," and "integration and international." Compare this with Rightworks (www.rightworks.com), also a made-up name, but one that conveys a clear message about this system integration company's objective of getting disparate B2B systems to work together.

Finally, a good brand must be able to work all over the world, since your B2B exchange may well be a global business.

Always bear in mind that the correct name is not the only factor in determining success or failure and providing the best customer care and support is much more important in building brand recognition and trust among users.

CUSTOMER CARE AND SUPPORT

A successful B2B exchange will spend the majority of its resources on building a strong customer care and support program in the early stages. In fact, sometimes it is justified to spend up to 80% of your resources on obtaining new members and keeping the existing ones happy.

First, the exchange must focus on its potential customers with targeted marketing campaigns, both direct mail and one-on-one presentations and demonstrations. Potential trading members are particularly essential in the early stages to build liquidity on the exchange.

Second, in addition to the usual marketing efforts to secure new members, a B2B exchange must have a thorough customer care and user support program for those people who sign up. The program must include at least:

- Regular training sessions that are free for members' staff;
- A 24–7 help desk, part or all of which can be outsourced;
- Trading desk support and trade facilitators to encourage new listings and trades—these staff must call members regularly to make sure they are using the system to its full advantage and encourage them to use it more;
- An organized system of receiving feedback from trading members;
- Dispute resolution mechanisms.

PREPARE FOR THE LONG HAUL

Dominance does not happen overnight. Indeed, if your exchange represents a paradigm shift for the industry, you must be prepared for a long haul in getting buy-in and wide usage. It took Catex two years of constant sales tours to persuade the traditionally conservative insurance industry that risk could be traded on a computer screen.

In our experience, the firm resistance to change that startup B2B exchanges encountered two years ago has now become a nervous acceptance within most companies that they must embrace the Internet and the changes it is bringing.

Many industries will argue that their business depends on personal contacts and face time. This process facilitates the development of intermediaries who can charge large commissions for bringing potential business partners together. In fact, though some industries resist the process more than others, no industry is unsuitable for automation of the transaction process through an on-line B2B exchange. Still, human interaction in signing up new members and encouraging them to use the new exchange's system is still very important in the early stages of growth.

CHAPTER SUMMARY

- Specialization means that there will be only one major winner in each vertical sector.
- The winner will take most in each vertical.
- Try to be one of the first to market in your vertical.
- If you are not dominating your market, look to merge with competitors. Winning as a B2B exchange is about domination; it is not about coming in second or third by avoiding dilution of your market share.

- Because liquidity is king for exchanges, you must build volume of trades as quickly as possible (for example, liquid stock exchanges always attract business from competitors).
- Build a critical mass of users as quickly as possible. A slow growth rate leads to loss of credibility.
- You need a massive marketing and customer care program to win converts quickly.
- Market share is worth more than profits in the early stages. For example, B2C valuation models are based on future revenue potential, not current net income.
- Once a winner has critical mass, there are very high barriers to entry for other exchange competitors.
- Building a great brand name is very helpful; for example, NYSE is the "Big Board," and Nasdaq has to compete with that image. But there is danger in having a name that is too restrictive.
- Don't fear other exchanges in the same industry if they are constrained from competing directly with you by regional geography or product characteristics.
- If your exchange represents a paradigm shift for the industry, be prepared for a long haul in getting buy-in and wide usage.

CHAPTER 11

Secret 3: Maintain Commercial Neutrality

Because an exchange provides a centralized market space for many competing members, both buyers and sellers, it must stay neutral in order to be credible and build trust.

The need for neutrality must permeate the whole exchange: the way it's designed, the way it operates, and the way it secures users' confidential information. The exchange's trading rules must not favor any single participant.

The exchange must be *perceived* as a neutral third party by all other parties, as well as actually acting as a neutral body, and it must be designed to benefit all the players in the industry that it serves.

The reason many B2B exchanges are being developed by people who have worked within an industry and are now leaving their Industrial Age corporations is that their former corporate employer would find it almost impossible to start an exchange, because of the neutrality issue. An exchange that is operated by or only for one particular player, or one particular class of user, will not be perceived as being independent.

STAY INDEPENDENT

Accordingly, it will be difficult to succeed if you are operated or controlled by just one user group, be it the buyers, the sellers, or the broker intermediaries in your chosen industry. Successful B2B exchanges must avoid becoming operated or controlled by one group of users or one company. This may not be easy, because as the exchange starts to succeed and grow, key strategic partners or specific user groups will seek to control you or a group of buyers or sellers may decide to work together to set up the exchange.

For example, several major steel mills took an equity interest in MetalSite at an early stage to ensure that their interests were represented in the development of the exchange. Similarly, the numerous industry consortia exchanges are primarily owned by one class of users.

If an exchange accepts investment by industry players, it must ensure that they do not achieve a control position and that their input is channeled through an independent process that ensures that all users' views are represented. An exchange that is set up by one class of users must be doubly sure that it operates in an independent and neutral way (see Chapter 16). In both cases, we recommend that the exchange set up an independent advisory board that can help counteract the purely commercial interests of that user group.

For example, when E. W. Blanche Holdings (www.ewb.com), a leading insurance broker, made an investment in Catex, the risk exchange went out of its way to ensure that it remained independent. In the press announcement on the investment, Catex stated that it had set up an independent board of governors to "oversee all functions of the exchange relating to neutrality and fair dealing."

In particular, a B2B exchange should avoid allowing the members to gain control, since they can restrict innovation to protect their existing businesses. As we discussed in Chapter 5, the world's largest stock exchanges have traditionally been owned and controlled by the broker members (for example, the NYSE, Nasdaq, and London Stock Exchange). In many cases, this has restricted the exchanges' ability to introduce more efficient trading mechanisms, such as a central limit order book with automated execution. As a direct result, these exchanges now face increasing competition from electronic communications networks (ECNs) and other trading systems that are sucking liquidity from the traditional stock exchange. The response of the management in these organizations, the world's three largest stock exchanges, has been to call for demutualization so that they can turn themselves into neutral, for-profit companies with a wide ownership structure and the flexibility to innovate and change their business models.

The lesson for B2B exchanges: Make sure you set yourself up as an independent, neutral party from day one.

AVOID PROPORTIONAL REPRESENTATION

As a successful B2B exchange develops and starts to dominate a particular industry, it will become increasingly important for it to represent all of the users of that market space. One way to achieve this is to partition the ownership between different user groups. For example, the exchange could reserve part of its shares for buyers, part for sellers, part for intermediaries, and part for the general public. In this way, it can be sure that all of the main user groups are properly represented in ownership and on the board of the company.

One danger of this approach is the temptation to develop proportional representation, whereby some user groups have greater voting rights than others. This arises because the largest user group argues that it should have the most say in how the exchange is run. To keep that user group in the exchange, the founders may agree to give them greater voting rights. However, in the long run, this is a recipe for disaster.

The only fair form of corporate governance is a "one share, one vote" system. In such a system, shareholders' influence is directly proportional to the amount of capital they have provided.

Certain governance issues raise regulatory concerns; these issues should be in the hands of an advisory board (see below).

The Chicago Board of Trade (CBOT) is a good example of how proportional representation can create a straitjacket for the exchange as the market grows. At its inception, the CBOT traded only agricultural futures contracts, such as wheat, corn, and soybeans. Originally, the liquidity in the CBOT's small commodity market came from the locals, that is, individual traders who were prepared to speculate on the price of such physical commodities. In 1975, the CBOT expanded to include financial contracts, including U.S. Treasury bond futures. As the derivatives markets grew, the financial products became the most popular and the world's largest banks, securities houses, and trading companies started to use them to hedge their risks or to make profits by speculating. The locals controlled the CBOT and they agreed to admit the big investment banks, to trade the financial derivatives, only if the locals retained the voting control. So they created a proportional representation system whereby the locals are full members and have one vote each and the firms that just want to trade the financial products are admitted only as associate members and have only one-sixth of one vote each. Since there are more than 1,400 full members and fewer than 900 associate members, the locals can effectively outvote the corporate members.

In today's global economy, financial derivatives are a critical part of the financial system and the U.S. Treasury bond future is the most actively traded contract in the world. However, the firms that provide most of the capital to support that trading do not have equal voting rights at the CBOT because of the historical legacy of control by the locals. In fact, the largest corporate dealers are so upset with the failure of the CBOT to innovate in the area of electronic trading and to merge their clearinghouse with the Chicago Mercantile Exchange that they announced their intention to explore the potential of establishing a completely new, fully electronic derivatives exchange in the United States. This clearly demonstrates how a proportional voting system that may make sense at one point in time is unlikely to remain a good idea as the exchange grows and expands its product base.

HAVE THE FLEXIBILITY TO MORPH THE BUSINESS PLAN

The B2B market space and the role of B2B exchanges in that space are dynamic. Although we try to provide some structure to the dynamics of this market space in this book, the world of business is now changing at Internet speed. This is why the cliché about the Internet heralding a revolution to surpass the Industrial Revolution is actually quite true. The result is that B2B exchanges must be incredibly light on their feet and able to innovate quickly.

Another cliché of the new economy is that your business plan should be morphed (that is, rewritten) every few months if you plan to stay ahead. This degree of flexibility is possible only in a highly entrepreneurial company that is not owned or controlled by Industrial Age structures.

Consider the dilemma faced by the management of Nasdaq. As we have discussed elsewhere in this book, Nasdaq succeeded by providing a market-making system to create liquidity in small company stocks. This made it an attractive market space for high-growth technology stocks, and many of those startups, such as Microsoft and Dell, went on to become hugely profitable companies. As they grew, the shares of these companies became extremely liquid in their own right and Nasdaq began to rival the NYSE for liquidity and volume traded. This encouraged the successful companies to stay listed on Nasdaq rather than move their listings to the "Big Board" of the NYSE, which had previously been the mark of ultimate success for a public company.

However, Nasdaq failed to reengineer the trading process for these types of stocks. Despite the management's attempts to introduce more efficient trading mechanisms, the members insisted on preserving the market-maker system, even though these types of stock are sufficiently liquid on their own. Because the market-making members owned and controlled Nasdaq, they were able to resist any significant innovation or morphing of the business plan. The market-making system is very profitable in liquid stocks because the market-makers are able to keep the bid–ask spread (the difference between the price they buy at and the price they sell at). This spread exists even though they are not taking much market risk because there are always lots of buyers and sellers (hence the natural liquidity). In addition, some market-makers colluded to keep the bid–ask spread as wide as possible, which ultimately resulted in regulatory action by the Securities and Exchange Commission.

The result has been that more efficient competitors, first Instinet and now nine other registered ECNs, have taken over 25% of Nasdaq's daily volume in the last two years. These ECNs are still pushing the envelope, introducing longer trading hours, international accounts for investors outside the United States, and other features. Forced to react to these competitive pressures, Nasdaq is looking to introduce a central limit order book, longer trading hours, and international alliances to create a global market space.

MAINTAIN THE CONFIDENTIALITY OF USERS' DATA

Successful B2B exchanges will build up an extremely valuable database of information about their chosen vertical market space. This data will include current prices, volumes, and trades but also historical prices and volumes (for example, what were competitors willing to pay for a product last month?) and product descriptions and details. Over time, this data will become a major component of the exchange's value proposition.

Determining who has access to the data is a significant issue for each exchange. Part of the confidential information that the exchange will build up includes sellers' product data and pricing, buyers' purchase history and price tolerance, and the financial records of members. All of this data must be secured in a way that ensures that a member's competitors cannot see it and requires the exchange to have secure systems.

It may be necessary to have an independent auditor review the systems and business practices of the exchange on a regular basis to provide potential members with an independent confirmation that their data will be kept securely. For example, MetalSite provides an independent report from Arthur Andersen LLP on the exchange's application of its core business principles, one of which is "Information Protection and Privacy: MetalSite maintains effective controls to provide assurance that individual buyer and seller information is treated in a highly confidential and secure manner."

INSTITUTE AN ADVISORY BOARD AND USER COMMITTEES

As an independent third party that provides a centralized market space tailored to the needs of a specific vertical market, a B2B exchange must ensure that all of its user groups are represented in the decision-making process.

The easiest way to achieve user representation in decision making, without a complicated ownership structure or weighted voting, is to institute an advisory board and set up committees comprising the different user groups.

The advisory board should include the highest-level industry representatives and highly credible analysts. The advisory board acts as a counterweight to the purely commercial interests of the shareholders and helps the exchange to be, and appear to be, a credible, neutral, and impartial marketplace. Within the exchange there should be a separate compliance team that reports directly to the advisory board. The compliance team is responsible for ensuring that the exchange's rules and regulations are observed by all members and are enforced fairly.

The advisory board should be a forum where the key players in the industry can provide input on policy without having a controlling ownership interest or control over the board of directors.

In addition, user groups are a perfect way for different users to have input.

One user group that all B2B exchanges should have is an executive management committee. This committee should be legally structured as a subcommittee of the board and should have certain powers delegated to it by the formal board of directors so that it can meet regularly and oversee the day-to-day operations of the whole exchange. This committee can have representatives from the management of key players in all the main user groups of the exchange. However, the firms they represent do not have to have any ownership or formal board representation in the company. This is particularly important when the exchange is majority owned by a particular group of users, as in an industry consortium, since it enables the exchange to operate in a neutral way despite the apparent bias in the ownership.

Another committee that all B2B exchanges must have is a systems user group to ensure that management is always receiving feedback on the web site and other information technology systems from the actual users. Another common user group is the trading and settlement committee, which should have representatives of the buyers,

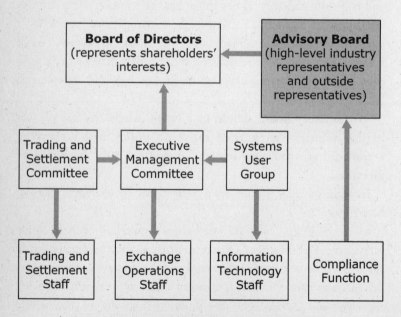

AN IDEAL COMMITTEE STRUCTURE FOR A B2B EXCHANGE.

sellers, and intermediaries and should approve the exchange's trading and settlement rules and regulations.

An ideal committee structure for a B2B exchange, based on our experience of running the BSX, is shown in the figure.

CHAPTER SUMMARY

- To be credible and build trust, exchanges need to stay neutral.
- An exchange must be both actually impartial and perceived as impartial.
- As you grow, strategic partners or specific user groups will seek to control you. Avoid becoming operated or controlled by one group of users or one company.
- Avoid letting members gain control, since they then restrict innovation to protect their existing businesses (for example, NYSE and other stock exchanges).
- You need to continue to innovate; your business plan must be fluid.
- Users' confidential information must be protected and not available to competitors.
- All user groups need to be represented in decision making—use advisory boards and user committees for this purpose.
- The advisory board should be a forum where the key players in the industry provide input on policy without having a controlling ownership interest or control over the board of directors. A compliance team within the exchange should report directly to the advisory board.

CHAPTER 12

Secret 4: Ensure Transparency and Integrity

Because an exchange provides a centralized market space for many competing members, it must be an open and fair market in order to be credible and gain the users' trust. A fair market is one that is transparent and built on integrity.

Some members may resist this if they believe that they can profit more from inefficiencies in the market (for example, a lack of pricing transparency). Successful exchanges will set and enforce market rules that do not favor any one user or group of users, even if they are owned by one user group, as in an industry consortium.

A good example of a fair exchange is MetalSite, which clearly states on its web site (www.metalsite.net) the following:

MetalSite is the premier electronic metals community where all interested parties can exchange information and goods through secure public and private channels. MetalSite's organization, policies and practices are structured to provide buyers and sellers of all types an unbiased and fair environment in which to conduct their day-to-day business.

MetalSite is a neutral market space for the exchange of goods and information among metal industry participants. MetalSite has created "Selling and Auction Rules" and a detailed "Privacy Policy" to communicate to our associates the guidelines and criteria by which our operations are conducted.

SELF-REGULATION

The exchange can ensure it is open and fair only if it is prepared to regulate the users of its centralized market facility. A B2B exchange should be a self-regulatory organization (SRO); an SRO imposes regulations on its own members and then enforces them through a strong compliance group.

Self-regulation is really enlightened self-interest, since it is always in the best interests of the exchange to maintain an open and fair market place.

Self-regulation should be contrasted with the alternative forms of regulation, which include regulation by an industrywide association or by a governmental body. Neither trade associations nor governmental bodies are sufficiently flexible to cope with the rapid development of the B2B market space. B2B exchanges should thus ensure that they keep their own house in order so as to avoid calls for outside regulation.

TRANSPARENCY

Transparency is a critical element of fairness and should be enforced by the exchange. At a minimum, all transactions made on the exchange should be reported to the exchange with full details on price and volumes. With fully automated execution, these details are immediately captured by the exchange's systems, but with post and browse and some auction-based exchanges the information must be given to the exchange by the parties to the trade.

The exchange should have rules and regulations that encourage transparency.

Different B2B exchanges will offer different degrees of transparency, depending on the balance they seek to strike between transparency and liquidity. For example, the London Stock Exchange lets market-makers delay disclosing large trades to the market to encourage them to provide liquidity in the market and to avoid the adverse price movements that could result from the immediate disclosure of their largest trading positions. On the other hand, most fully electronic trading systems provide immediate (but anonymous) disclosure of every trade.

Pricing transparency creates a more efficient market, which often leads to lower prices. For example, in the reinsurance industry it is currently common for a large reinsurer to depend on an insurance broker to introduce business. This means that the broker controls the information about who is buying reinsurance and at what price. Since the industry is dominated by around four large brokers, those brokers control the flow of pricing information, and the clients of one broker may not know what the clients of another broker are paying for the same product. The introduction of Catex is leading to screen-based trading of risks and enabling buyers and sellers of risk to meet each other through a neutral B2B exchange. The premium price paid (called the "rate on line") for all trades made on Catex is posted on the web site at www.catex.com. For the first time, there is a degree of pricing transparency in the reinsurance market.

Full disclosure is the mantra of a fair and open exchange.

Transparency also applies to the products traded through the exchange's systems. Sellers must disclose full information about the items they are selling to enable buyers to make a reasoned assessment of the true value of the products. The exchange should therefore enable sellers to put full product specifications and details on the web site. Buyers will not return to a market where they purchase a pig in a poke.

INTEGRITY

The centralized pricing system is the most important function of an exchange, and the exchange must seek to ensure the integrity of that pricing mechanism. The following are the key elements of a fair system:

- Access is equal for all.
- The order with the best price has highest priority.
- First in, first out (FIFO).
- Effective procedures ensure that each seller's products are posted correctly and that buyer bids and orders are transmitted accurately.
- Trades are consistently executed in accordance with the published rules of the exchange.

Equal access means that every trading member has equal access to the exchange's trading system, irrespective of size or duration of membership. Price priority means that any new order that offers a better price takes priority over existing orders. (That is, the lowest ask or the highest bid price takes priority over other orders with a less attractive price.) FIFO means that when orders have the same price, the time of entry of an order sets the priority of that order, with the first order received by the exchange taking priority over subsequent orders received at that price. With a fully electronic, automatching system, these rules can be hard-wired into the system software using sophisticated algorithms.

To the extent that the exchange's trading rules cannot be hard-wired into the trading system, the exchange must introduce and enforce the trading rules against the members. The rules of a successful B2B exchange will require members to honor the integrity of the exchange's pricing mechanism. Members must agree not to do anything that will hinder or disrupt the fair and orderly functioning of the market. This should include a requirement that traders will not seek to manipulate the market, either on their own or through collusion with other members (for example, by spreading false information, misleading others about the true position of the market, or creating false trades to give the appearance of activity). All of these practices have a long and infamous history in the world of securities trading, and stock exchanges around the world have formed trade associations that issue standards of best practice and core principles for exchanges to implement.

Finally, members should be under a general obligation not to mislead or deceive customers in advertising goods or services through the exchange or completing transactions through the exchange's systems.

THE EXCHANGE'S GATEKEEPER ROLE

To maintain credibility and trust, an exchange must regulate access to its centralized market space. In implementing this concept, the exchange must decide what standards and qualifications it will impose for joining the exchange and for continued membership. In all cases, the firm and its relevant employees should be fit and proper persons without any record of dishonest or fraudulent trading activities.

In a post and browse model, the exchange provides a form of members' room where buyers and sellers meet. To make such a mechanism effective and ensure the integrity of the system, the exchange must prequalify entrants to the members' room. At least the exchange must ensure that they are legally able to buy or sell in that market and that they have some interest in buying or selling what is offered on that exchange. In an auction-based exchange, the exchange must also ensure that the sellers are acceptable to the buyer for a reverse auction (for example, with respect to the quality of their products and creditworthiness) or that the buyers are acceptable to the seller for a normal auction.

In an automatching environment, the exchange must seek to ensure that buyers and sellers who are anonymously matched in the system can conclude the trade. Too many failed trades will destroy the credibility and integrity of the exchange. This may require the exchange to impose financial responsibility rules on members (for example, requiring members to have a minimum level of paid-up capital, liquid assets, or credit rating from an independent third party). Members must then be required to monitor and calculate their financial position with sufficient regularity to ensure that they remain in compliance with the exchange's minimum capital requirements.

There may also be wider regulatory issues to consider, particularly if the exchange trades products that are securities or commodities contracts. For example, CreditTrade enforces strict controls on who can access the trading portion of its site. In the United Kingdom, the Financial Services Authority regulates the activities on the Credit-Trade site and not only has established certain minimum standards of eligibility for trader access but also requires regular reporting.

CORNERING THE MARKET

The exchange must seek to prevent the market's being dominated or cornered by any one user group.

One of the most infamous attempts to corner a market involved the Hunt brothers of Texas in 1979–1980. In 1979, the two Texas oilmen started amassing silver, much of it with borrowed money, in an attempt to corner the market. And they did corner it for a while, driving the price from $10 an ounce in 1979 to a high of $52 an ounce in January of the following year. At that price, people flooded the market with an excess of silver. When the price dropped, the Hunts' loans were called and they had to sell. On 27 March 1980— later dubbed Silver Thursday—the Hunt brothers' attempt to corner the silver market finally ended. The price of silver plunged to $10.80 an ounce from $21.62 an ounce the day before, a 50% single-day decline. This incident alone is often cited as justification for the heavy regulation of the commodities markets that now exists in the United States under the Commodities Exchange Act.

You should avoid setting up a B2B exchange for markets that are dominated by a small number of suppliers or by one big buyer that can dictate the price. For example, the market for semiconductors is dominated by a small number of suppliers, such as Intel, and is not suitable for a B2B exchange.

STANDARDIZATION

One of the value propositions of an exchange as opposed to an unregulated telephone market lies in the standardization of the product, the legal environment, the trading and settlement terms, and the documentation.

A successful B2B exchange will draw up rules (or encourage members to adopt existing industry standards) that regulate the quality of the products offered on the exchange, the lot sizes in which they are offered, the way in which they are priced, the acceptable pricing increments (called the "tick size"), and the standard terms for trading and settlement. Many of these rules may be varied by agreement between the parties, but every trading member of the exchange should know that in the absence of specific terms, the standard terms set by the exchange will apply.

Regulating the quality of the products offered on the exchange helps to build trust in the exchange's centralized market space. Similarly, creating standardized documents and a common legal environment helps an exchange avoid disputes and earn a reputation for integrity.

COMPLAINTS AND DISPUTE RESOLUTION

As members of a community, the members of the exchange should be required to honor the just and equitable principles of conduct set out in the exchange's rules and commonly practiced in the market space where they are conducting business. This should include a requirement to honor the trading obligations to one another that arise from trading on the exchange.

Successful B2B exchanges will provide a mechanism, formal or informal, for prompt and orderly resolution of complaints from and disputes between trading members.

Since B2B exchanges are Internet businesses, it makes sense for the dispute resolution process to be an arbitration forum, set up in accordance with the International Arbitration Standards and accessible on-line (that is, with documents filed and arguments presented on-line).

SYSTEMS INTEGRITY

The exchange must ensure that all of its systems are robust to avoid systemic failures. As users become dependent on the exchange for pricing, trading, and data it becomes more and more essential to provide fully redundant, highly secure systems. In the B2C space, the bad publicity eBay got after several well-publicized outages of its core systems demonstrates graphically the dangers of system failures for a B2B exchange.

Security of data on the exchange's systems must be high (for example, through the use of serious levels of encryption) to build up the members' trust. Members must be satisfied that their confidential data is secure within the exchange and there can be no unauthorized use of that information.

POTENTIAL GOVERNMENTAL REGULATION OF EXCHANGES

If a B2B exchange becomes dominant in a marketplace it may raise public pressure to regulate the operations of that marketplace. For example, as PaperExchange becomes the dominant price-setting mechanism for paper products worldwide, the prices determined on PaperExchange will affect every business and every household product that uses paper (for example, the daily newspaper). This could lead to the belief that such an important B2B exchange should be required to operate for the public good, rather than purely as a private-sector, for-profit initiative.

This national interest ingredient may encourage the belief that some B2B exchanges should operate as quasipublic utilities rather than purely as private-sector, for-profit initiatives.

The securities markets are a classic example of such calls for regulation. Regulation of stock markets in the United States came shortly after the 1929 Crash. Before the Crash, stock prices rose swiftly and steadily thanks to a post–World War I boom and new and growing industries such as aviation, radio, and motion pictures. For the first time, the general public took a keen interest in trading. To become involved, however, many small investors had to borrow money. When the price of stocks plummeted in 1929, these investors went bankrupt trying to repay loans. Many companies, too, went out of business from lack of capital.

In the early 1930s, the U.S. Congress sought to stabilize and regulate the securities marketplace by enacting two new laws: the Securities Act of 1933 and the Securities Act of 1934. The first requires that securities offered through interstate commerce or the postal system must be registered with the federal government before public sale. It also requires that relevant financial information about the issuing company be made available to potential investors through a document called a "prospectus." The second law created the Securities and Exchange Commission (SEC) and provided additional protective measures, such as prohibiting misrepresentation, manipulation, and other abusive activities. The SEC's primary responsibility was—and still is—to administer the 1933 and 1934 acts. The 1934 act also provides that any company that operates a national stock market in the United States must be registered as such with the SEC.

B2B exchanges must adopt sound self-regulatory practices to avoid calls for legislation to regulate and license their activities as national markets once they become dominant in their industry.

CHAPTER SUMMARY

- B2B exchanges need to maintain an open and fair market to build credibility.
- There is a critical need for transparency in pricing and the product—this creates efficiencies and leads to lower prices. Some user groups may resist this.
- B2B exchanges need to maintain the integrity of the pricing mechanism.
- B2B exchanges need to regulate members' activities and adopt a members-only-room approach that includes prequalifying members.
- B2B exchanges must prevent the market's being dominated or cornered by any one user group.
- To build trust in the market, B2B exchanges need to regulate product standards.
- B2B exchanges need to create or encourage the use of existing standardized contract terms to ensure integrity and avoid disputes.
- B2B exchanges must ensure that their systems are robust to avoid systemic failures—security must be high (for example, through the use of encryption) to build trust.
- Successful B2B exchanges may be seen as quasipublic utilities and elicit calls for government regulation, as happened to the U.S. securities markets after the 1929 Crash.

CHAPTER 13

Secret 5: Add Value by Building a Virtual Community

Although an exchange's primary function is to provide a centralized pricing mechanism and market space, successful B2B exchanges will grow beyond this and develop into full-fledged exchange communities. They will provide the services that allow people in the same vertical to network effectively and access all the business information they require in one place.

In their ground-breaking book *Net Gain: Expanding Markets through Virtual Communities,* John Hagel III and Arthur G. Armstrong made the following observation:

> The rise of virtual communities in on-line networks has set in motion an unprecedented shift in power from vendors of goods and services to the customers who buy them. Vendors who understand this transfer of power and choose to capitalize on it by organizing virtual communities will be richly rewarded with both peerless customer loyalty and impressive economic returns. But the race to establish the virtual

community belongs to the swift: those who move quickly and aggressively will gain—and likely hold—the advantage.

In 1997, when they wrote those words, the main impact of the Internet and virtual communities had been in the B2C and C2C spaces. Most businesses were not embracing the Internet, and the first B2B exchanges were just being set up. Accordingly, their insights were mainly made in the context of on-line, consumer-oriented communities. However, their insights about setting up virtual communities apply equally to B2B applications.

Successful B2B exchanges will become powerful virtual communities.

THE SIX Cs OF ON-LINE SERVICES

Steve Case, the CEO of America Online, is famous partly for identifying the "Six Cs" that make up a complete on-line service:

- Content,
- Context,
- Community,
- Communications,
- Connectivity,
- Commerce.

B2B exchanges must build in all of these factors to create a valuable trading community:

Commerce—the centralized market space;
Content—trading data, pricing, product information, industry-specific news, and so forth;
Context—specialization in a vertical;

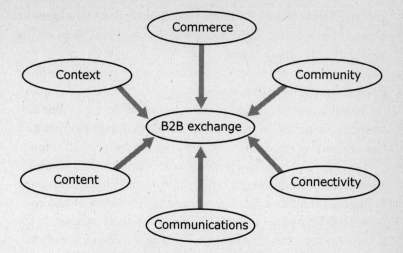

**B2B EXCHANGES MUST BUILD IN STEVE CASE'S
"SIX CS" OF ON-LINE SERVICE.**

Community—value-added services that attract and hold new
users;

Communications—the ability for members to meet each other
and communicate with each other on-line;

Connectivity—use of open, web-based applications so that members can use the Internet to connect to the exchange.

It is critical that a B2B exchange not try to build its own network
but rather ensures that all its systems are on the Internet and offers its
trading mechanism on the world wide web, since these are open systems that are accessible by all.

ESTABLISHING A TRADING COMMUNITY

The first thing an exchange needs to establish is the appropriate trading mechanism (see Chapter 5). This may be a catalog aggregator, a

post and browse model, an auction mechanism, or a fully electronic automatching system. **This centralized market space must be the exchange's core competency.**

Next the exchange needs to focus on signing up as many users as possible, as quickly as possible.

Only then can the exchange add value by building a community. However, in all cases it is important for the exchange to expand on this core market space capability as quickly as possible.

The order of these stages is the direct reverse of the B2C and C2C community models, where it is necessary to establish the community before the members are likely to transact between themselves.

With B2B exchange communities, the initial magnet is the commerce function. The community then develops around that.

In the process of signing up users, we have identified the need to smother potential users and signed-up members with customer care and support (see Chapter 10). Excellent customer care is critical in establishing the strength of your brand, creating user loyalty, and thus building a sense of community.

In *Net Gain,* Hagel and Armstrong identified three stages of entry in building a community and reaching a revenue-earning position. The first "gate" a virtual community must pass through is generating traffic, that is, getting target community members to travel to your site. For a B2B exchange, this stage entails establishing the trading mechanism and signing up members to trade in the centralized market space.

The second gate is concentrating traffic, that is, getting members to spend increasing time in the community. For B2B exchanges, this stage requires the addition of community services that engage the trading members and add value for them, such as

- Fostering relationships and networking between industry players;

- Aggregating trading data, organizing news feeds, and accumulating member-generated content.

The third gate identified by Hagel and Armstrong is locking in traffic, or creating switching barriers that make it increasingly difficult for members to leave the exchange community. For a B2B exchange, this third stage involves

- Expanding the exchange's functionality by providing access to third-party services, such as analytical research tools and historical data;
- Tailoring the exchange community to individual members' needs by allowing them to customize their experience;
- Integrating member firms' back-office systems with the exchange or providing back-office logistics within the exchange's web site.

THE ECONOMICS OF MEMBERS AS CUSTOMERS

As a B2B exchange builds the value of its community and starts to lock members into its services, the lifetime value of a member as a customer increases. This means that the revenue stream for the exchange from a member over the lifetime of its membership goes up as the exchange develops into a community.

Conversely, the costs of attracting new customers (members) will fall sharply as the exchange develops its community. The law of increasing returns means that the exchange with a critical mass of liquidity will attract more new buyers, which attracts new sellers, and so on (see Chapter 10), without having to increase its marketing or other costs of acquiring new members.

As the lifetime value of each member increases faster and the costs of customer acquisition fall faster, the profit margins

of the dominant B2B exchanges will be far higher than in the off-line world.

ENHANCING THE COMMUNITY SERVICES OF A B2B EXCHANGE

The elements of a B2B exchange community are similar to those that have worked in the B2C and C2C space—after all, businesses are run and managed by individuals—but the focus is on supporting those individuals when they make business decisions rather than influencing their personal spending or lifestyles. The following are some services that can be added to a B2B exchange.

Industry Rolodex. The primary aim of the community service is to enable users in the same vertical space to network together. In the physical world, this normally occurs through specialist magazines, trade shows, and conferences. The B2B exchange can supplement, and even usurp, all of these physical mechanisms. Successful exchanges will add member communication services so that your exchange's address book becomes the Rolodex for your vertical market sector.

News Feeds. Another aim of an exchange community is to give managers all the business information they require to do business in that specific vertical through one central resource and to help them process that information efficiently. This is done by supplying customized news feeds that are industry specific (for example, weather forecasts for commodity producers and shipping news for import and export markets). MetalSite, for example, provides news and columns from *American Metal Market, Metal Center News,* and *New Steel.*

Directory of Relevant Services and Resources. Organized directories of links to other resources on the Network and of buyers, sellers, and intermediaries will assist members of the exchange community.

Scrolling Ticker. A scrolling ticker displays new bids and offers, postings, trade information, and transaction prices, as well as news headlines in real time. No exchange worth its salt doesn't have a scrolling ticker.

Bulletin Board. In addition to any trading bulletin board, a general bulletin board for business networking is often a well-used feature and results in member-generated content.

Discussion Forums. Having empowered buyers through the centralized trading mechanism, it will also be important to allow them to communicate with each other to share experiences and pass on knowledge gained from dealing with different suppliers. MetalSite, for example, provides discussion forums that are restricted to registered members only. Again this creates member-generated content. These forums should be structured as threaded forums that are monitored by a customer care professional.

Industry Newsletters. The exchange should support its users by producing a customized newsletter every month, including interesting articles from other publications, and by sending members e-mail messages to alert them to key new information.

Calendar of Industry Events. For example, PaperExchange has an industry calendar of events.

Job Search and Job Ads. PaperExchange enables users to post job listings and résumés, and PlasticsNet maintains a career center.

Classified Ads. Classifieds add to the networking opportunity on the site. PlasticsNet has an active classifieds section for members.

BECOMING THE "BLOOMBERG" TERMINAL IN YOUR VERTICAL

In his autobiography *Bloomberg by Bloomberg,* Michael Bloomberg tells the fascinating story of how he set up Bloomberg Financial Services and quickly grew the company into the leading information vendor in the world. At least part of his success is due to his initial focus on the trading of bonds (fixed income securities). Within this vertical, Michael had many years of experience, including being a partner and head of information systems at Salomon Brothers, the large investment bank and bond dealer in New York. Bloomberg developed his terminals with all the historical data, real-time prices, news feeds, and yield curve analysis that the average bond dealer required to be able to trade effectively. Accordingly, bond-dealing rooms from New York to Hong Kong could be set up around the Bloomberg terminals as the primary information and dealing system.

A B2B exchange should aim to make its web site the "Bloomberg terminal" for its particular vertical. To do this, the exchange first must ensure that all real-time pricing and trading data from its centralized market space is readily available to members. This is accomplished by having a scrolling ticker on the site and adding customized e-mail alerts that advise members when new prices are posted or trades have been made (wireless application protocol technology now allows such alerts to appear on a user's mobile phone).

Second, the exchange must add streaming news services that are tailored to the needs of traders in its particular vertical. For example, Catex provides a news flash on any major insured catastrophe and provides a special weather tracking service. In the future, it could add live news feeds with the latest information and pictures of any insured disasters.

Third, the exchange should build up a database with historical pricing information and provide analytics and research. Analytics are the analytical services that traders require to be able to trade more efficiently. These may be specialized pricing models that allow traders to construct theoretical prices (for example, a Black-Scholes pricing model for options or derivatives) or test different trading strategies (for example, if they buy so much of product X, how much of product Y must they buy?). Research is professional analysis of the market and market trends that can help buyers and sellers assess where the market is headed.

DOCUMENTS CENTER

One way to add value and at the same time lock in members is to standardize the contract terms, terminology, and documents used on the exchange in order to grow the market. Incorporating a "documents extranet facility" into the web site can do this. In this facility, members can post documents for others to access, work on revisions to the contract documents, and download documents to their own computers. Sophisticated documents extranets

- Allow a posting party to specify which other users can see or amend a document on the system;
- Automatically alert those people that there is a document up there for them;
- Track revisions and changes;
- Inform the posting party when other users access the documents;
- Provide a library with precedent documents and templates that can be used by members.

By providing precedent documents and helping members draw up contractual documents on its web site, the exchange can steer the industry toward more standardized forms and terms. At the same time, it can help an exchange lock in members while building barriers to entry for any potential competitors.

Finally, for complex transactions, a secure collaboration communications service such as IntraLinks's DealSpace will greatly assist two parties in closing their trade.

MEMBERSHIP DATABASE

To improve the community and customize a user's experience, you need to build and maintain a member database. This starts with the system profile that each user is required to complete when they set themselves up as a member and user of the system. Over time, the member database can extend to monitor the user's use of the exchange.

One way to encourage use of the system is to reward members who trade a lot, for example, by assigning them star ratings within the system, and allow users to rate other members. This way, other members see which firms or traders are the "stars" of your exchange and know that members' contributions are acknowledged.

LOGISTICS AND SYSTEMS INTEGRATION

In addition to the centralized market space, a B2B exchange can offer various centralized back-office and logistics systems or arrange to host members' systems on its central hardware.

In the securities world, some smaller stock exchanges have purchased a fully automated middle-and back-office brokerage system that they operate on behalf of their broker members. This enables new trading members to get up and running quickly, since they do not have to buy their own systems, and ensures that they are committed to the exchange.

For B2B exchanges that trade physical products, this can include providing invoicing, accounting, and purchase-order generation services. Enabling users to ship goods, track orders and handle all the logistics of delivery on-line through the web-site will also help them into your exchange.

SOPHISTICATED FINANCIAL SERVICES

As the exchange develops, more sophisticated financial services can be added, such as

- Credit for buyers;
- Credit analysis, enhancement, or insurance for sellers;
- Payment processing;
- Receivables management;
- Insurance or warranties;
- Shipping, warehousing, and inspection services;
- Political risk insurance for international trades;
- Foreign currency services to minimize currency risk.

SOPHISTICATED SECURITIES
LIKE DERIVATIVES

Successful B2B exchanges can create indices and develop derivative products that help members hedge their physical positions or protect themselves from future price changes. These new products increase the attraction of the exchange to existing members and widen the potential user groups to include investment banks, alternative investment managers, and speculative securities traders.

The first indices can be a historical weighted average of all transactions completed on the exchange for a specific product or term or with respect to a given region. Initially, the indices should be calculated for the most commonly traded product or combination of products within each category or region. Once an index has been developed, it can be traded in the form of an options or futures contract in which the value of the derivative contract is based on the level of the index at a specific future time.

For example, Catex may be able to create catastrophe risk indices based on the prices of a given type of reinsurance deal made in their system and to license those indices to insurance companies, investment banks, or derivatives exchanges for the trading of options or futures contracts. Those derivative contracts would enable the reinsuring companies to hedge their exposure on the underlying reinsurance contracts.

As the United States deregulates electricity along the lines of the European model, electricity may become one of the most actively traded commodities. In this vertical, HoustonStreet and Altra Technology are vying for market dominance. Traders deal in electricity on a wholesale basis, buying it from power producers and selling it to local utilities or to investors who take speculative positions. Each megawatt hour (MWH) produced gets traded many times before it is consumed. Electricity prices can swing from $10 to $1,000 per MWH, depending on the temperature, the time of day, and TV viewing habits, such as usage peaks when the whole nation is watching the Super Bowl on TV. To smooth out these huge price spikes, producers must manage the risk using derivatives with active participation from major financial market-makers.

HoustonStreet is developing Forward Physical Electricity Contracts, which enable power producers to hedge their expo-

sure to sudden and dramatic shifts in the price of electricity based on unforeseeable variables such as weather changes or catastrophic events.

This will be a purely financial market for price hedging, risk management, and trade in forward and future power contracts. The trading time horizon is up to three or more years; contracts can be divided into weeks, blocks, seasons, and years.

ACCESSING CONTENT

Since time to market is critical, a B2B exchange shouldn't delay its launch until it has all of these community services fully developed. It should launch the basic trading service and seek to buy in or add as many of them as possible, as quickly as possible. Examples of third-party service providers are

- Networking, forum, scheduling, and other "groupware" services (for example, Realcommunities.com);
- Customized news feeds (Bloomberg, Reuters, and industry-specific news sources);
- Logistics and supply chain management (such as RightWorks .com and Logistics.com);
- Escrow services (such as Tradenable.com);
- Credit analysis (for example, ecredit.com);
- Document management (such as IntraLinks.com);
- Personalized stock tickers (for example, Yahoo! Finance on PaperExchange.com).

In addition, member-generated content is critical to building a sense of ownership and involvement among users. Member-generated content will come through the addition of bulletin boards, threaded discussion forums, and communication services. A B2B exchange should also hold regular meetings of the user groups (see Chapter 12) to get feedback on its systems and community functions.

CHAPTER SUMMARY

- Successful B2B exchanges will be powerful virtual communities.
- Start off by establishing the trading mechanism for the centralized market space (for example, post and browse or auction).
- Sign up as many users as possible as quickly as possible. Then add value by building a community.
- Smother the users with customer support.
- Add member communication services such as a Rolodex for your vertical market sector, customized news feeds, bulletin boards, and discussion forums.
- Make your web site the central information source for your market space—become the "Bloomberg terminal" for your vertical by providing customized news and information services and by adding transaction data, product information, background analysis, and access to analytics.
- Build a documents facility: standardize contract terms, terminology, and documents used in order to grow the market.
- Link in users' back-office systems or provide those logistics services through your exchange's web site.
- Create indices and develop derivative products that help users hedge their physical positions (for example, stock exchanges have created equity indices).
- Hold regular user group meetings to get feedback on the systems.

CHAPTER 14

Secret 6: Make the Right Strategic Partnerships

The universality and ease of use of the Internet mean that people no longer have to gather on one physical trading floor to create liquidity. However, a new B2B exchange can challenge an entrenched Industrial Age market only if it builds liquidity at a much lower cost. Increasingly cheap computing power and telecommunications are the weapons that allow Internet-based trading networks to challenge traditional trading mechanisms.

However, the successful exchange must be able to build that liquidity quickly and expand to meet the demand in Internet time. By far the easiest way to achieve this, as proven by the successful B2C applications, is to work with strategic partners from the very beginning. **Choosing the right strategic partners helps you scale up quickly toward domination.**

POTENTIAL PARTNERS

Potential partners for a B2B exchange are deep-pocket investors, buyers in the chosen market space, sellers, existing broker intermediaries, new infomediaries, content providers, information technology (IT) vendors, and trading systems software developers.

However, as we emphasize in Chapter 11, it is critical for the exchange to remain commercially neutral and that no one user group (for example, buyers, sellers, or existing brokers) is able to control the operation of the market.

e-STEEL is a good example of a successful partnership with an IT vendor. After spending months developing the proper business model, e-STEEL chose Computer Sciences Corporation (CSC) as a strategy and technology partner and began a nine-month site development.

Another good example of a successful partnership with an IT vendor is Catex. The founders of Catex had insurance industry experience but lacked the IT knowledge to design and build an electronic system for trading risk. To plug this gap, they approached Science Applications International Corporation (SAIC), an employee-owned software giant that is one of the largest software companies in the United States. SAIC had previously designed and built an exchange for trading sulphur dioxide emission certificates, and, since they own Network Solutions (the "dotcom people"), they come with strong Internet credentials. SAIC became an equity partner in Catex and designed and built the original Internet-based trading system for Catex.

CreditTrade is an example of a successful partnership with a trading system software vendor. In this case, the software house Mutant Technology came up with the idea to build an Internet-based trading system for credit derivatives and, using its CEO's prior experience as head of structured derivatives trading at Barclays De Zoette Wedd, launched CreditTrade.

MetalSite has grown quickly in the steel industry by attracting a number of large steel producers as strategic partners. These sellers made an equity investment that provided essential capital, but they also brought with them the added liquidity of their business and the credibility that comes from endorsement by key industry players. For example, Bethlehem Steel Corporation, the second largest integrated steel producer in the United States, joined MetalSite in September 1999. Bethlehem Steel obtained an equity interest in MetalSite and in return brought significant tonnage and additional product lines to MetalSite.

CLICKS AND MORTAR PARTNERSHIPS

In seeking to dominate an on-line vertical, some B2B exchanges may find it necessary to form a strategic partnership with a traditional bricks and mortar company. Such an alliance has been called a "clicks and mortar" model.

For example, CreditTrade, the on-line credit trading exchange, has joined forces with Prebon Yamane, a leading global credit derivatives intermediary, to provide traders with greater access to real-time data, improved trading information, and enhanced liquidity via the Internet. Under the agreement, Prebon Yamane moved its global credit derivatives team (the bricks and mortar) and historical default swap database to CreditTrade in return for a substantial equity stake. In all, 13 credit derivatives brokers in London, New York, and Singapore joined CreditTrade's on-line credit sales desk to form a single global team. The agreement highlights the potential benefits to all market users of combining the personal attention provided by traditional voice brokers with the speed, efficiency, and cost-effectiveness of an Internet B2B exchange.

Similarly, CheMatch (www.chematch.com), a leading bulk chemicals and fuel products exchange, recently acquired The Energy Group (TEG). TEG is a traditional petrochemical feedstock and gasoline components brokerage firm based in Houston, Texas. In a press release, Larry McAfee, president of CheMatch.com, states, "TEG will substantially increase the liquidity on the CheMatch platform, particularly in the feedstock products. . . . With TEG's experience in the financial derivatives market this acquisition should accelerate our OTC derivatives activity and provide our customers with better risk management tools."

If an independent exchange faces competition from an industry consortium exchange, it may well make sense for the two exchanges to merge and combine the natural liquidity of the consortium with the independence of the entrepreneurial exchange.

CUSTOMIZE THE MARKET

As part of the laserlike focus that is required to dominate a particular vertical, a successful B2B exchange must tailor its applications to the specific needs of its chosen market space. **The best way to achieve this is to work closely with the potentially big users of the exchange and get inside their heads.**

VERTICAL KNOWLEDGE

Many B2B exchanges are being developed by experienced vertical industry professionals who see that, with Internet technologies now being adopted by business, there is an enormous opportunity for them to start up a B2B exchange. These professionals typically have deep knowledge of their particular industry and strong relationships with the main buyers and sellers in that vertical space. Alternatively, exchanges are being set up by existing market participants through industry consortia. In both cases, the vertical knowledge is critical to building credibility for the exchange within that vertical quickly and to ensure that the exchange tailors itself to that particular market.

If a B2B exchange does not have the necessary level of vertical knowledge on day one, it must move quickly to secure such expertise. This can be achieved by buying in the experience or by establishing a strategic partnership with a group that does have the vertical knowledge. After some initial success, the founders of PaperExchange realized the critical need for sound vertical knowledge and secured a strategic partnership with Roger Stone, a leading industry figure. Stone became an investor and the chairman of the exchange.

An exchange's vertical knowledge and early sign-up of key industry players are major barriers to entry for potential competitors and ensure that the law of increasing returns applies to that exchange.

OUTSOURCE THE TECHNOLOGY

We strongly advise the builders of B2B exchanges to outsource the technology development. It is critical for a successful B2B exchange to focus on its core competency—the specific industry expertise that will enable it to create the best business solution possible for that market space—and let the outside technology experts build the systems.

Although we recommend the outsourcing of the technology build, we also highly recommend that a B2B exchange buys in the IT expertise of a strong chief technology officer (CTO). One of the dangers faced by all companies in the new economy is the potential to be

"Amazoned." By this we mean the potential for an established business to be blindsided by a new technology that appears, apparently out of nowhere, and enables completely new startups to invade a market space quickly. This is what Amazon.com did to bricks and mortar retail bookstore chains in the mid-1990s. An experienced CTO can manage the outside vendors in the systems buildout and, at the same time, keep a weather eye out for any tectonic technology shifts.

For three years, B2B exchanges had to build their own systems because third-party options were not available. In the last two years, however, a rash of startups have rushed to build and sell the technology for on-line auctions and other exchange functions. Prominent among them are Ariba, Commerce One, Moai Technologies, i2 Technologies, and RightWorks. In addition, some of the specialist stock exchange system vendors, such as OptiMark Technologies, EFA Software, OM Systems, Living-systems.com, and Computershare, are now seeing the opportunity to refocus their industrial-strength trading and matching engines on other B2B exchange applications.

Many opportunities have been spawned by the growth of B2B exchanges, such as providing technology, marketing, connectivity, content, and consulting services to these new exchanges.

NEW AGE THINKING

In the Industrial Age, a common approach to project development by companies was to start by engaging a large firm of outside consultants. The methodology behind this approach was based largely on the belief that it is a mistake to take key senior executives away from their existing jobs to develop a new project. Moreover, an outside firm of consultants can approach all interested parties (including potential competitors) and come up with an independent view.

This approach is not ideally suited to the development of B2B exchanges, which need to

- Emerge and launch in Internet time;
- Have entrepreneurial leadership and be flexible;
- Be designed as neutral third-party applications rather than as units within an existing industry player;
- Have sound vertical knowledge and hands-on industry expertise.

INFOMEDIARIES

One of the most obvious areas for an emerging B2B exchange to seek strategic partners is in the development of community services (see Chapter 13). Since an exchange's core competency is the centralized trading facility, it is unlikely that the exchange will initially have either the resources or the experience to develop many of the potential add-on services that a full community requires.

Sources of reliable historical market data are key potential partners. The value of a trading facility is greatly enhanced by the availability of market data, such as historical prices, volumes, and analytical research services. This content will develop on the exchange itself as it grows, but in the early stages it may be necessary to buy in the data from the existing traditional market space.

CHAPTER SUMMARY

- Strategic partners help you scale up quickly toward domination.
- Potential partners include deep-pocket investors, buyers in the chosen market space, sellers, existing broker intermediaries,

new infomediaries, content providers, IT vendors, and trading systems software developers.

- Get inside the heads of big users to tailor the market to their specific needs.
- Buy in industry-specific expertise if necessary.
- Buy in technology awareness to avoid being "Amazoned" by new technology.
- Outsource the technology build.
- Avoid large teams of consultants.
- Partner with infomediaries who already have data (for example, historical trade data for securities).

CHAPTER 15

Secret 7: Operate as a Virtual Corporation

In the new economy the winners will be flexible corporate structures that can morph their business plans and innovate in real time.

In the B2C environment we have seen the business model shift dramatically at least three times in the last four years. First companies sought to charge subscriptions for content on the web. Then the concept of free content developed, together with attempts to create "portals" that aggregate "eyeballs," with revenue being generated by advertising. Now the emphasis is on driving e-commerce transactions through these portals.

In the United Kingdom, the classic business model of America Online, charging monthly subscription fees for Internet access and premium content, has been effectively challenged by free Internet service providers, such as Dixon's Freeserve. Now even the staid British Telecom is offering free Internet access. To counter these threats, AOL has had to morph its business plan overnight and offer its own free Internet service in Europe.

In the same way, the B2B space is evolving rapidly, and only those companies that are light on their feet will be able to survive.

B2B exchange companies must be able to move quickly, innovate, and scale up fast.

Since B2B exchanges are a new species of B2B application, the founders of these companies have the opportunity to start with a clean sheet and adopt the best practices of Internet startups. Invariably this means that B2B exchanges should be "virtual corporations."

ANATOMY OF A VIRTUAL CORPORATION

There are eight key guidelines for virtual corporations:

1. Concentrate on core competencies. Build the right central market space with a trading mechanism that is tailored to your chosen vertical (see Chapter 6).
2. Outsource the rest. Choose the right strategic partners, who can add value to your core competency (see Chapter 14), or third-party vendors who will provide additional services through your exchange.
3. Remain flexible at all times. In part this means having teams run the business and adopting virtual communications instead of face-to-face meetings.
4. Keep staffing levels low. This is sometimes the most difficult part of being a virtual corporation, but if you outsource vigorously it is possible to keep the full-time staff on the payroll to a minimum. Key full-time staff should include a chief executive officer, chief operating officer, chief financial officer, sales and marketing head, customer support head, and smart chief technology officer to manage the outsourced IT vendors.
5. Plan to operate on a 24–7 basis. In e-commerce you must be able to operate around the clock, unlike bricks and mortar businesses, which operate 9 to 5.

6. Choose professional advisors who specialize in Internet startups. An important first step in launching a B2B exchange is obtaining first-class legal and accounting advice on the design of the market, the rules and regulations of the exchange, and the legal documents for transactions made on the exchange. Choose a top firm of accountants as auditors, but pressure them to accept low fees for their audit services in the early years. Don't worry about them; they'll do very well for fees if and when you go public. Some service providers and consultants may accept equity in lieu of fees in the startup phase.
7. Build partnerships with key corporate leaders.
8. Develop strong funding support.

OUTSOURCE, OUTSOURCE, OUTSOURCE

If your staff are to be able to concentrate on the core competency of quickly building a customized trading facility, they cannot be distracted by the need to add other services to the exchange. Outsource everything else, including

- Technology build;
- Addition of content and community services;
- Provision of logistics and document processing.

THINK PRIVATE, ACT PUBLIC

Smart Internet entrepreneurs establish their businesses as limited-liability private companies but act as if they are publicly listed companies from day one.

In the United States, publicly listed companies have to have filed a full registration statement with the Securities and Exchange Commission (SEC), conducted an initial public offering (IPO), and been accepted for listing by the NYSE or Nasdaq.

Acting like a publicly listed company means that you should prepare to go public from day one. This approach includes

- Hiring the best lawyers and accountants with experience in taking an Internet company public;
- Forming tier 1 relationships;
- Having annual audits on your financial statements from the end of the first year;
- Having a proper board of directors with an audit committee and a compensation committee;
- Setting up a strong, independent advisory board.

Forming tier 1 relationships and choosing top professional advisors are critical to building confidence in the exchange and developing the credibility and integrity of the exchange.

B2B exchanges that want public exposure before conducting an IPO in the United States can list on the Mezzanine Market (www.mezzmarket.com) of the Bermuda Stock Exchange (BSX). (Full disclosure: The authors are, respectively, the former chairman and the current CEO of the BSX.) The Mezzanine Market on the BSX is designed specifically for e-commerce and technology companies to be publicly listed on a recognized stock exchange without having to register their securities with the U.S. SEC and conduct a full IPO to retail investors. Instead, investment in the Mezzanine Market is restricted to accredited investors—essentially institutions (such as venture capital funds) and high-net-worth individuals. Listing on the Mezzanine Market gives a company the profile of a public corporation while also giving it time to grow until it is sufficiently large enough to justify a full IPO in the United States and a listing on Nasdaq or the NYSE. The Mezzanine Market thus offers an interim stage when the company's securities are essentially a form of listed, private equity.

CUSTOMER CARE

Exchanges have many types of customers, and they all demand a high level of attention. Successful exchanges must focus on marketing to potential customers, since new trading members are particularly essential in the early stages in order to build liquidity on the exchange.

In addition to the usual marketing efforts to secure new members, an exchange must have a thorough customer care and user support program. This must include regular training sessions, a 24–7 help desk, and trading desk facilitators to encourage new listings and trades. These critical employees must get very close to the members and help them to use the system to their maximum benefit, and ensure that all the members use the system regularly.

JURISDICTION SHOPPING

As an Internet-based application, B2B exchanges must be prepared to position themselves as global players from day one. Given that revenues are likely to be generated from all over the world, it makes sense to start off by incorporating a holding company in a leading neutral jurisdiction like Bermuda. Bermuda companies are internationally recognized, and Bermuda is an ideal, neutral jurisdiction that is acceptable to business users all over the world. Bermuda is also a leader in its early adoption of an Electronic Transactions Act in 1999, which creates complete certainty as to the legal validity of contracts formed electronically through web sites such as a B2B exchange's system.

FUNDING OPTIONS FOR B2B EXCHANGES

As with all Internet and e-commerce startups, the initial capital for a B2B exchange will probably come from the three Fs—family, friends, and fools!

After that, the first and second financing rounds are critical. You must try to choose financial partners who have deep pockets, so that you can tap those partners for the serious money quickly when you need to scale up later.

To avoid "down rounds" after missed budgets, don't make your business plans too optimistic on revenues. Venture capitalists (VCs) always build in "ratchet provisions" that can dilute founders significantly in a down round.

When seeking venture capital, always remember what a VC looks for in a B2B exchange:

- A monster market—but avoid markets that have few buyers or are dominated by a few sellers (for example, the market for semiconductors, which is dominated by Intel and IBM);
- Management experience, including a high level of specific vertical knowledge;
- A market with a complex, fragmented supply chain that a B2B exchange can simplify;
- A market where buyers and sellers are willing to use technology to create more efficient links between them;
- Speed to market (do you have first-mover advantage?);
- Scalability;
- A business model that works, with revenues.

CHAPTER SUMMARY

- B2B exchange companies must be able to move quickly, innovate, and scale up fast.
- Concentrate on your core competencies.
- Outsource, outsource, then outsource the rest.
- Keep staffing levels low.
- Prepare to go public from day one. Hire the best lawyers and accountants and form tier 1 relationships.
- Have annual audits. Choose professional advisors who specialize in Internet startups and accept equity in the early days in lieu of fees. Force auditors to accept low fees at the start; they will do fine if you go public.
- Outsource the technology.
- Find a smart CTO to manage the outsource vendors.
- Focus on the customers with targeted marketing.
- After family, friends, and fools have invested, try to choose financial partners who have deep pockets. Have the ability to tap partners for the serious money quickly when you need to scale up.
- Business plans should not be too optimistic on revenues to avoid "down rounds" after missed budgets.

Part IV

THE FUTURE OF B2B

CHAPTER 16

Entrepreneurs versus Industry Consortia

As we emphasize in Chapter 10, *liquidity is king* for B2B exchanges, and so a successful exchange must get the largest number of buyers and sellers and ensure that the largest buyers and the largest sellers use its central market space. Two different approaches to this issue are currently being explored.

ENTREPRENEURIAL MARKETS

Many B2B exchanges are being developed as independent dotcoms by experienced vertical industry professionals who have seized the opportunity for them to leave their Industrial Age corporations and start up a B2B exchange. Their former corporate employer would find this difficult to do on their own because of the perceived lack of neutrality when a major player owns the market space. These entrepreneurs have a deep knowledge of their particular industry and strong relationships with the main buyers and sellers in that vertical space.

Entrepreneurial exchanges have the following advantages:

- Perceived neutrality.
- Speed—quick decision making is essential.
- Independence.
- A dedicated and motivated professional CEO/management team.
- The ability to refine and change the business model in real time. A good example here is AviationX, which started out as the B2B exchange for the whole aviation industry. However, when several major airlines announced their own consortia approach, AviationX was nimble enough to refocus on smaller regional airlines and adjust its business plan to make it more of an application services provider for them.

However, all dotcom exchanges have to raise enough capital to survive the long buildup phase, and some of them have not made it. In addition, dotcom exchanges need to acquire sufficient liquidity to make them a winner. One way to do this is to attract the largest buyers and sellers to the exchange with special deals, such as reduced fees or an equity stake. This has raised some questions about the continuing neutrality of these exchanges.

We believe that a dotcom exchange must embrace the biggest buyers and sellers in its market space, and this may require it to provide some equity shares. As long as the exchange continues to operate as a neutral market and retains the other elements of neutrality that we highlight in Chapter 11, such as objective standards for new members, fair and equal access to the trading system, and an independent compliance team that reports directly to the advisory board, the exchange can still demonstrate the necessary level of neutrality to attract other players.

On the other hand, providing exclusive access to a small number of suppliers or buyers is often a bridge too far and will deter other key players from joining the exchange.

INDUSTRY CONSORTIA

Not to be left out of the B2B revolution, a number of large bricks and mortar companies have decided to form their own B2B exchanges. Competitive pressures are now forcing even the largest manufacturers to work together to launch B2B exchanges. For example, GM, Ford, DaimlerChrysler, Nissan, and Renault are working together to create an auto exchange called Covisint. These types of exchange are being called "industry consortia plays," because they are formed by a consortium of existing buyers or sellers in a particular market space. There are now more than 40 such industry consortia plays. Leading ones include

Exostar—Boeing, BAE Systems, Lockheed Martin, and Raytheon in the aerospace and defense industries.

MyAircraft—United Technologies and Honeywell International in the aerospace industry.

GlobalNetXchange—Carrefour Supermarche, Sears Roebuck, Kroger, and J. Sainsbury in the retail supermarket space.

WorldWide Retail Exchange—a B2B retail store procurement exchange being set up by Target, Kmart, Safeway, Walgreen, DairyFarm, and 13 others.

e2open—Acer, IBM, Hitachi, Matsushita, LG Electronics, Nortel Networks, Seagate Technology, Solectron, and Toshiba in the computer, electronics, and telecommunications industries.

Transoria—a consumer products exchange (food, beverages, and household consumable products, mainly) being set up by a large number of the leading consumer brand manufacturers.

These consortia plays are representative of either the buy side or the sell side. In either case, they have the major advantage that they are well funded by their bricks and mortar parents. However, these attempts to start a B2B exchange face the same challenges the entrepreneurial ones face. In particular they must

- Play to win. Liquidity is king, and the exchange with the most trading will dominate.
- Operate as a neutral exchange, so they attract the maximum number of potential buyers and sellers to generate the most efficient prices.
- Operate as a virtual company, so they can be fast and flexible and change the business plan quickly.

An enormous advantage for consortia plays is that they bring tremendous natural liquidity to the exchange in the form of combined buying or selling power. The largest problem that consortia face is how to establish the operating neutrality of the exchange. One of the most hotly debated issues in B2B is whether consortia plays can retain sufficient neutrality to attract other buyers and sellers.

The key issue is not necessarily ownership but how the exchange is operated and controlled. Independent ownership and neutrality in operation are not the same thing.

The main things that an industry consortium must do to demonstrate its neutrality are

- Establish objective standards for new members.
- Maintain fair and equal access to the trading system.
- Appoint an independent CEO and management team with entrepreneurial incentives to develop the exchange.
- Have an advisory board and user committee structure (as described in Chapter 11) that brings representatives from all the user groups into the management of the exchange.
- Set up an independent compliance team that reports directly to the advisory board and enforces the exchange's rules and regulations fairly against all members.

Every industry consortium must be staffed with dedicated, independent management. Right now, most industry consortia are seconding existing staff into these proposed new exchanges. This generally doesn't work well. The seconded staff do not have the right motivations to make the business succeed—even at the cost of some of the owners' core existing businesses. Similarly, seconded staff do not tend to have the "career at risk" or bottom-line responsibility that would motivate them to change the business plan as frequently and as dramatically as may be required to succeed.

THE UPCOMING CONVERGENCE

We believe that there will now be a period of intense competition between entrepreneurial B2B exchanges and industry consortia plays in various vertical markets. Ultimately, however, the winner-takes-most effect will drive mergers and consolidations, and one dominant exchange—the one with the greatest liquidity—will emerge in each vertical.

B2B exchanges are being judged on how well they serve all their members and how fair and equal they are. The winner is likely to be the exchange that demonstrates that it is operated in a neutral way so that all buyers and sellers feel comfortable in joining that market.

CHAPTER 17

Antitrust Issues

In Chapter 2 we identified the potential for these many-to-many markets to bring together buyers and sellers from all around the world. The results can be a highly competitive virtual market in which on-line auctions create dynamic pricing, reducing manufacturers' costs of raw materials, parts, and supplies. In addition, these net markets have the capability to link the manufacturer with its suppliers (tier 1) and its suppliers' suppliers (tiers 2 and 3). This can lead to greater efficiencies in the design of products and ultimately to a "build to order" business model that dramatically reduces manufacturing time, inventory levels, and distribution costs.

On the other hand, we accept that virtual markets can still create the opportunity for collusion, unreasonable restraint of trade, abuse of market power, and, in the case of exchanges led by the buy side, the power to drive purchase prices below free-market prices (that is, monopsony power).

PROCOMPETITIVE STRUCTURAL FEATURES

There are a number of structural features that we believe can help ensure that these dynamic new businesses create the significant procompetitive efficiencies they promise to deliver.

Trading system design

The new feature of all these B2B exchanges is that they are using the ubiquitous connectivity standards of the Internet to enable companies to connect to each other, to connect to the exchange's central market, and to power their electronic trading systems. By definition, no B2B exchange has a physical trading floor or relies on brokers' communicating by telephone or fax to execute trades.

As a result, B2B exchanges have electronic pricing mechanisms that provide a full audit trail of all activity in the system and can be hard-wired to ensure that anticompetitive activities do not occur on the exchange.

As we state in Chapter 12, the centralized pricing system is the most important function of an exchange and the exchange must ensure the system's integrity. The following are the key elements of a fair system:

- Access is equal for all.
- The order with the best price has highest priority.
- First in, first out (FIFO).
- Effective procedures ensure that each seller's products are posted correctly and that buyers' bids and orders are transmitted accurately.
- Trades are consistently executed in accordance with the published rules of the exchange.

With a fully electronic, automatching system, these rules can be hard-wired into the system software by sophisticated algorithms. The rules of a successful B2B exchange will require members to honor the integrity of the exchange's pricing mechanism.

To the extent that the exchange's trading rules cannot be hard-wired into the trading system, the exchange must introduce and enforce the trading rules against the members.

Ownership structure

Most traditional stock exchanges, such as the NYSE and London Stock Exchange, were set up by stockbrokers and are still owned exclusively by brokers. Such exchanges operate rather like a "mutual society" or private club.

It was mainly because the NYSE acted as a private club that the U.S. government passed the Securities Exchange Act of 1934, which requires all national securities markets to be registered by the Securities and Exchange Commission. For example, in the 1920s the NYSE protected long-standing members who were trading while insolvent, rather than kicking them out immediately.

In contrast, B2B exchanges are being set up as for-profit, neutral market spaces. This follows from their objective of bringing as many buyers and sellers together as possible to create dynamic pricing and thereby lower the cost of procuring supplies for buyers and expand the range of potential buyers for the suppliers. Some are being set up by independent entrepreneurs, such as the Stojka brothers, who founded PlasticsNet. Some are being set up by a group of large players in that industry; for example, MetalSite was set up by Weirton Steel, LTV Steel, and Steel Dynamics, and Covisint is being set up by a group of the largest auto manufacturers. In all cases they are seeking to be neutral and independent markets with access open to all players in that industry.

B2B exchanges that are truly open have objective criteria to determine who may have access to the centralized, electronic marketplace and provide equal access. Equal access means that every trading member has equal access to the exchange's trading system, irrespective of size or duration of membership.

MONOPSONY POWER

As we've said, the main objective of B2B exchanges is to bring together more buyers and sellers to create dynamic pricing and thus lower the cost of procuring supplies. They empower the buyers by enabling them to contact more potential suppliers and creating the potential for reverse auctions, in which the buyer sets a price and the suppliers bid on it (with prices falling as the auction progresses). They also benefit suppliers, because sellers from all over the world can access the whole range of potential buyers for their products. The use of traditional auctions allows the sellers to get buyers to bid competitively for their products.

What is fascinating about the Internet revolution in B2B e-commerce is that it has created a historic shift in the balance of power from the supplier to the buyer. This is illustrated by the industry consortia that are being formed by the buy side. These buy-side consortia are combining their procurement operations to create a central, on-line marketplace. In each case you have a group of buyers realizing that in the networked economy they can lower their procurement costs by creating a central exchange. In these B2B exchanges all the potentially suitable suppliers can link to the exchange electronically over the Internet and the buyers can create dynamic pricing by getting those suppliers to bid in on-line auctions for some contracts (reverse auctions).

On the other hand, by combining their purchasing power through an exchange and restricting suppliers' access to it, the buyers may be able to exercise monopsony power and force the suppliers who are members to quote prices below those that would prevail in a freely competitive market. This danger is more prevalent in industries that are already dominated by a small number of large purchasers than in industries that are more fragmented.

However, providing these B2B exchanges are set up as for-profit commercial entities with open access, they would be in breach of their financial responsibility to maximize shareholder value if they were to subjectively restrict access to their markets. Imagine if the World-Wide Retail Exchange, the B2B retail store procurement exchange being set up by Target, Kmart, Safeway, Walgreen, and DairyFarm, among others (www.worldwideretailexchange.org), decided to restrict access to a limited number of suitable suppliers/vendors. It would be self-defeating.

Initially, the retailers might be able to extract cost savings from the vendors they admitted, but by limiting access to a small number of potentially suitable suppliers, the retailers would actually be reducing their chances of securing food, drugs, general merchandise, and textiles of the right quality at a lower price and with the right after-sales service, etc. In such a scenario, the retailers would risk driving their limited number of selected suppliers to depress output and ultimately to go out of business as they forced the prices down. Open market forces therefore dictate that this B2B retail store exchange will be open to the widest range of potential suppliers that prove they can deliver goods of the quality, in the quantity, and with the other service attributes that the retail stores require.

CONCLUSION

Calls for nascent B2B exchanges to be regulated are premature, in our opinion. One reason why the Internet has been the driving force in the new economy and helped improve U.S. productivity is that the U.S. government has taken a relatively hands-off approach in both regulation and taxation. B2B exchanges are still at a very early stage of development and should not be burdened with overregulation.

The key issue is that B2B exchanges can increase competition and promote efficiency and should be given the opportunity to prove that. The Internet has created a historic shift in the balance of power from the supplier to the buyer. In the face of such a dramatic reversal of the economic metrics, it would be detrimental to rush in and apply Industrial Age regulatory structures to emerging B2B e-markets. It is free markets, low barriers to entry, and easy access to startup capital—and not governmental regulation—that will ensure that all B2B exchanges preserve open and equal access to their market spaces.

Moreover, many B2B exchanges are also global, so any regulation, which we do not recommend at this time, would need to be coordinated with other major governments in Brussels and Tokyo.

We therefore hope that the Federal Trade Commision (FTC) in the United States and the European Union will refrain from premature regulation. This appears likely. After conducting a thorough investigation of Covisint, the exchange being created by an industry consortium of automakers, the FTC has decided to allow it to proceed. (We submitted a written comment to the FTC during its June 2000 public workshop, "Competition Policy in the World of B2B Electronic Marketplaces," which was prompted by the formation of Covisint.)

However, we also believe that regulators should maintain a watching brief to ensure that successful B2B exchanges do not change their open structures to support anticompetitive features. At this stage, regulators should focus their attention on marketplaces where there is already a concentration of power in a small number of bricks and mortar buyers or sellers rather than on the more fragmented markets.

CHAPTER 18

2B or Not 2B On-Line?

Every business must now ask itself, "2B or not 2B on-line?" That is the question.

The answer?

"Yes!"

The Internet is helping corporate America reinvent itself and has undoubtedly contributed to five of the last nine years of continuous expansion in the U.S. economy. Outside the United States, companies all over the world are beginning to integrate the Internet into everything they do. In a study by Booz Allen & Hamilton and the Economist Intelligence Unit entitled "Competing in the Digital Age: How the Internet Will Transform Business," 92% of senior managers at five hundred large companies worldwide said they believe the Internet will transform their business and reshape world markets by 2001, and 49% indicated that the Internet will have a major impact on their market by 2001.

At times of tectonic shift, everything is revisited and analyzed to see if it can be reinvented. Right now, companies are reviewing how they buy and sell from each other, how they communicate with each other, and how they distribute their products to new businesses. In this brainstorming blizzard, B2B exchanges are well positioned to become central to all forms of B2B e-commerce.

For companies considering the Internet's role in their industry, a dominant B2B exchange will be the killer application that lowers their purchasing costs, reduces their inventory levels, and helps them keep track of their orders and expand their market globally.

SIZE OF THE MARKET

In the first edition of this book we predicted that the total B2B market space in the United States alone will hit $1.5 trillion by 2004. This overall total includes the value of the infrastructure builders—such as the software companies—and the individual storefronts that the largest manufacturers will be able to maintain, as well as the value that will pass through B2B exchanges (as we have defined them).

At least 40% of this trade value will be captured by B2B exchanges within the next four years, which means that the total value of all transactions made through B2B exchanges in the United States alone will exceed $600 billion by 2004.

The Gartner Group has added some weight to our original prediction by estimating that worldwide e-commerce will reach $7.29 trillion in 2004, of which at least 37% will be accounted for by B2B e-markets.

If B2B exchanges capture revenues representing just 0.5% of the $600 billion turnover that we predict, they will collectively generate $3 billion in revenue per annum by 2004—and that's just in the United States! Leading analysts believe that the gross margins of B2B exchanges will be as high as 85%, so they should represent an enormous investment opportunity in the longer term.

THE INTERNET *IS* THE STRATEGY

Even the largest and oldest multinationals in the world are now engaged in a headlong rush to integrate the Internet into everything they do. Many of the best-known industrial companies have appointed high-level strategic think tanks to try to ensure that they are not "Amazoned" by an Internet-savvy startup. Jack Welch, the 63-year-old chairman of General Electric, is now reinventing GE from top to bottom under the mantra "destroyyourbusiness.com." Every division of GE now has a full-time "dyb" team whose task is to reinvent their division's business around the Internet before someone else does.

For all companies, the Internet should be more than just a communications system. Integrating the Internet into everything it does should be every company's strategy.

For some companies this means setting up new units to transfer their products and services on-line. Often these new dotcom units will actually compete with the Industrial Age divisions, but they are critical to ensure that the whole company does not get left behind. For example, Federal Express has an internal unit that is building a totally Internet-based logistics-information system to enable companies to communicate more effectively with their suppliers, customers, and shippers. If this new unit is successful, it will undoubtedly reduce the amount of information that currently gets passed around between those parties using traditional FedEx courier packages.

For other companies, this means spreading their bets and investing in various Internet-based businesses in the hope that one or more of their investments will pay off. For example, in the U.S. securities markets, the largest trading members of the NYSE are now busily investing in multiple electronic communications networks (ECNs) and proprietary trading systems. The ECN Archipelago Holdings, for example, lists Goldman Sachs, Merrill Lynch, JP Morgan, Instinet, and E*Trade as investors. At the same time, Goldman Sachs and Merrill Lynch are invested in Brass Utility and Primex, two competing ECNs, and in OptiMark Technologies, and Goldman Sachs owns more than 16% of Wit Capital. E*Trade is an electronic broker, and Instinet is a form of ECN; interestingly, Instinet is also invested in Tradepoint, an emerging ECN in the United Kingdom.

In this environment, B2B exchanges are ideally placed to secure serious investors. Both Internet-focused venture capital firms and Industrial Age companies that missed out on the B2C dotcom phenomenon are now exploring B2B opportunities on the Internet.

However, key to the success of any B2B exchange is maintaining operating neutrality.

NETWORK MEGATRENDS

Underlying the rapid penetration of the Internet into businesses in the United States and across the world are two Internet-enabled megatrends. The first is Kevin Kelly's new law of networks, as he sets down in his book *New Rules for the New Economy*. The second is a shift in power from sellers to buyers.

In the new economy, the value of a network like the Internet actually increases faster than Bob Metcalfe's formula of n^2, where n is the number of people connected. Kelly has pointed out that on an electronic network we can make multiple simultaneous connections between groups of people, so that the potential value of the network is not just $n \times n$, but n^n.

B2B exchanges are the most dynamic example of this type of network, since many buyers and sellers can come together and communicate with each other in a virtual trading space.

The second megatrend is a shift in the balance of power to the customer. In the B2B world, the Internet has created a historic shift in power from the companies selling products to the companies buying those products.

B2B exchanges are the killer application in this Internet Revolution and are creating the dynamic pricing that enables buying companies to significantly lower their acquisition and procurement costs, lower their inventory levels, and ensure more on-time deliveries to their customers.

GROWTH AREAS AND CONSOLIDATION

The next year will see a proliferation of new B2B exchanges. Some will compete with, and improve on, the existing exchanges in markets like steel, paper, credit derivatives, electricity, and insurance. Others will be launched in completely new markets. Look for new and existing B2B exchanges to achieve prominence in industries that have large gross revenues of which a substantial part is currently going to distributors, brokers, or intermediaries. It is these markets that will see the most changes as B2B exchanges develop and enable the manufacturers to avoid much of the intermediaries' fees and the high costs of distribution. For example, PaperExchange has been very successful in the paper industry (a $600 billion gross revenue market in the United States alone) because it is a fragmented market in which the profit margins of the distributors are higher than those of the paper manufacturers.

As we point out throughout this book, not all exchanges in the same vertical can succeed. The need to dominate and win in a specific vertical will drive many of these competing new entrants to merge.

We therefore predict a period of rapid new growth (12 to 18 months) followed by a period of mergers (18 to 36 months). The merger of PaperExchange and MPX Inc. is a sign of the mergers to come.

EXPANSION

Successful B2B exchanges will dominate their chosen vertical markets and then seek to expand into other, closely related vertical spaces.

If the verticals are closely related, there will be obvious advantages in amortizing the exchange's infrastructure across two or more markets. For example, CommerX is now looking to transfer its experiences in developing PlasticsNet to other related verticals, and MetalSite has announced plans to expand from steel products into metals such as aluminum, copper, and zinc.

As B2B exchanges grow, they will also create private markets for large buyers or direct buyer-supplier connections, leveraging the exchange's core trading technologies. The development of a private network enables an exchange to charge a monthly administration fee and forges strategic relationships with key industry players. Exchanges such as BigMachines, Catex, and CreditTrade are already setting up and operating private networks for their members, and we see this as a growing trend among B2B exchanges.

B2B EXCHANGE NETWORKING

We maintain a web site at www.b2bexchanges.com where we offer updates on the information in this book and a networking association for B2B exchanges and interested corporations worldwide.

FEED THE PLENTITUDE.

Kelly's third law of the new economy states that "plentitude, not scarcity" governs the network economy, by which he means that the more networks you are connected to, the more value you can create. With b2bexchanges.com we are trying to maximize the number of relationships flowing between successful B2B exchanges.

In the same vein, companies are realizing that they need to be connected to multiple B2B exchanges to access all the goods and services they require—from traditional supplies for maintenance, repairs, and operations (MRO) to the raw materials they use to manufacture consumer products. Over time, B2B exchanges in different verticals will evolve common standards and seek to link themselves together and integrate their systems, creating an even more valuable network.

THE FUTURE OF THE SECURITIES INDUSTRY

In the securities industry we will see a continuing drive toward global trading. This is most likely to come about through the electronic trading networks' linking together to create a swarm, rather than through mergers of traditional stock exchanges. There are too many conflicting agendas, such as systems, personalities, and nationalist feelings, for traditional national stock exchanges to work well together. Many of these electronic trading networks will be launched by international broker-dealers who wish to internalize their own order flow and then feed any outstanding orders into a centralized limit order book maintained in an electronic matching engine.

A good example of this new trend is the deal between Credit Lyonnais Securities Asia (CLSA), a leading non-U.S. broker-dealer, and Bloomberg Financial Markets, which operates a U.S. ECN called "B Trade." Under this agreement, CLSA will feed their international, non-U.S. order flow into a global ECN called "G Trade." In this new environment, electronic trading systems will be ideally positioned to become global ECNs in niche markets. For example, the Bermuda Stock Exchange is positioning itself as a well-regulated global ECN for the electronic matching of trades in securities that are not registered with the U.S. SEC (such as the shares of hedge funds and other alternative investment vehicles). Traditional stock exchanges will find it increasingly difficult to compete with these electronic trading networks as they link together to form global networks, and, to survive, the old stock and commodities exchanges will have to rapidly reinvent themselves as demutualized, for-profit, entrepreneurial companies.

These electronic global trading systems will eventually evolve into multiproduct platforms, providing markets to trade derivatives fixed income and traditional equities globally, all on the same system.

All industries should take note of the fundamental reshaping of the securities business that the Internet and a few order-matching computers have wrought.

OPPORTUNITIES FOR ELECTRONIC TRADING SYSTEMS

Among the opportunities being created by the proliferation of B2B exchanges are the licensing and sale of electronic trading systems to the exchanges. In this space, the securities market specialists are well ahead of the software firms, such as Ariba and CommerceOne, which are currently developing systems for B2B exchanges. Expect to see firms like EFA Software, OptiMark Technologies, and OM Systems—who are providers of sophisticated automatching trading systems—moving aggressively into the B2B exchange market space.

As James Martin points out in his new book, *After the Internet: Alien Intelligence,* software is now being designed in ways that allow the program to evolve and develop a form of machine, or artificial, intelligence. In the near future, rather than humans, sophisticated software agents with artificial intelligence will conduct on-line trading on B2B exchanges.

In the B2B space, everything is in play. B2B exchanges are the killer application of this Internet-based revolution for businesses. May the best exchange win in each vertical!

CHAPTER SUMMARY

■ The Internet is helping corporate America reinvent itself and has undoubtedly contributed to five of the last nine years of continuous expansion in the U.S. economy.

- We predict that B2B exchange transactions will exceed $600 billion by 2004 in the United States alone, with a potential revenue of at least $3 billion per annum.

- All businesses must reinvent themselves around the Internet (as GE is doing). The Internet is more than just a communications medium; it must become the main business strategy.

- Metcalfe's law of networks has been replaced by Kelly's new law of networks (n^n). B2B exchanges are the most dynamic example of this type of electronic network, since many buyers and sellers come together and communicate with each other in a virtual trading space.

- In the present environment, B2B exchanges are ideally placed to secure serious investors from Internet-focused venture capital firms that missed out on the B2C dotcom phenomenon and Industrial Age companies that are exploring the Internet.

- Winner takes most. Consolidation is likely as competing exchanges seek to dominate.

- Successful B2B exchanges will branch out into complementary verticals and also set up and run private networks for members.

- Feed the plentitude. Successful B2B exchanges will link and integrate their systems with other B2B exchanges to create a more valuable network.

- At our web site, www.b2b.exchanges.com, we update the information in this book.

- In the future the securities industry will see electronic trading systems and broker-dealers linked together to create a swarm. Traditional stock exchanges will have to reinvent themselves to survive.

- Securities trading system software companies will move into the general B2B exchange space.

- In the B2B space, everything is in play.

Appendix

SELECTED COMPANY PROFILES

BigMachines.com

Catastrophe Risk Exchange (CATEX.com)

CreditTrade.com

e-Chemicals.com

e-STEEL.com

MetalSite.net

NTE.com (formerly the National
Transportation Exchange)

PaperExchange.com

TechEx.com

BigMachines.com

OVERVIEW

BigMachines.com is the leading provider of hosted Internet applications to enable e-business for engineered systems. By powering an industrial machinery manufacturer's web site and connecting to multiple marketplaces, the BigMachines.com Internet Sales Channel offers a complete solution for selling new, engineered machinery and parts on the web. The company also hosts the BigMachines.com Marketplace, a global, neutral market for new, engineered machinery and parts. The BigMachines.com technology enables product selection and configuration based on engineering requirements. The company has integrated this selection and configuration technology with a complete e-business engine that enables engineering collaboration, request-for-quotes (RFQ) buying, and direct buying.

HISTORY

BigMachines.com was founded on 1 January 2000, by Godard Abel, Goerdt Abel, Vic Alston, Eugene Chiu, Christopher Shutts, and

Sculley Brothers LLC. Godard Abel first recognized the inefficiencies in the selling process for complex, engineered products while consulting for industrial machinery companies at McKinsey & Company. After attending Stanford Business School and becoming general manager of iNiku.com, the Internet business portal for Niku Corporation (Nasdaq: NIKU), Godard saw the opportunity to develop a hosted, web-based application for the $1 trillion machinery industry to sell complex, engineered products via the Internet. He rapidly brought together a founding team with experience in Internet startup, software development, and machinery engineering. The Abel family, who ran ABEL Pumps, brought over fifty years of industry experience and relationships in Europe and the United States. BigMachines.com is a privately held company funded by investments from its founders, Sculley Brothers LLC, the Kraft Group, and other industry and Internet leaders.

VERTICAL MARKET OPPORTUNITY

The bulk of the $1 trillion annual sales in the industrial and commercial machinery industry is engineered and configured for specific applications. This huge market was not being addressed by existing B2B solutions, which focus on commodities; catalogues; maintenance, repairs, and operations products; used/surplus items; and direct materials. Engineered machinery is built to order and thus requires a tailored selection and configuration technology to enable online collaboration and e-commerce.

Both sellers and buyers of industrial machinery face significant challenges. To find the machinery best suited to a specific application, many parties must collaborate across multiple companies. Manufacturers have tremendous internal sales costs, driven by internal engineering groups who manually assist their external sales force, distributors, and potential buyers through the complex machinery selection and configuration process required for customer quoting and order generation. The engineering and bidding processes are slow and expensive, with many redundant loops of verbal communication and paper processing. Errors are made in machinery selection that result in lost orders, inferior machinery performance, and high service and warranty costs. Moreover, sellers had great difficulty in reaching potential customers around the world.

To address these industry needs, BigMachines.com developed hosted Internet applications to enable e-business for engineered systems and to revolutionize the selling of complex, engineered products via the Internet. These applications combined machinery-specific selection and configuration with an end-to-end "eCommerce" engine with RFQ and direct-order capabilities. BigMachines.com rapidly assembled a world-class team that combined industrial machinery experts with cutting-edge Silicon Valley Internet developers. The founding and management team holds B2B Internet and e-commerce startup experience from Niku Corporation, Extricity, and Andale. The team also has extensive experience in the industrial machinery industry at Bechtel, Fluor Daniel, Case Corporation, General Electric, Goulds Pumps, Ingersoll Rand, and McKinsey & Company.

MEMBERSHIP MODEL

BigMachines.com is a neutral company owned by private investors. Membership in the BigMachines.com Marketplace is limited to qualified buyers and sellers of industrial machinery. Sellers of industrial machinery must also have their catalogs of new, engineered machinery and parts made available on the web by BigMachines.com.

TRADING MODEL

BigMachines.com provides an end-to-end e-commerce solution to industrial machinery companies through its hosted Internet applications for selling new, engineered machinery and parts. The BigMachines.com Internet Sales Channel offers a complete on-line sales network that includes a direct "eSales" solution, the BigMachines.com Marketplace, and interfaces to multiple exchanges and procurement technology platforms. The BigMachines.com eSales solution powers a supplier's web site with a customized, cobranded selection, configuration, and e-commerce functionality. It automates the supplier's sales process based on their products and customer base, creating a private market exclusively for their goods. The BigMachines.com solution can be fully integrated with back-end enterprise resource planning systems and is accessible through third-party enterprise procurement applications. The company also provides extensive professional services and support for implementation, technology integration, and e-business strategy. Through the combination of the BigMachines.com Marketplace and direct eSales, suppliers gain a new customer channel that increases margins and ensures their survival in the Internet economy.

The BigMachines.com Marketplace aggregates multiple suppliers and incorporates transaction-ready content as well as commerce services such as transaction processing, bid management, and directory services to provide one-stop shopping to large industry buyers. After machinery selection and configuration, buyers can place RFQs and create purchase orders for new machinery directly through the BigMachines.com Marketplace or eSales solutions. Machinery parts can also be directly ordered or quoted after the BigMachines.com system dynamically generates a machine's unique bill of materials. In the future, BigMachines.com may create private markets for large buyers or direct buyer-supplier connections, leveraging the BigMachines.com technology. BigMachines.com will focus on automating the manufacturing sales transaction cycle to reduce and more accurately determine lead times from all of a buyer's suppliers.

MARKET ENTRY STRATEGY

BigMachines.com has initially targeted industrial machinery sellers to web-enable their product offerings and power their existing web sites with the BigMachines.com's eSales solution. BigMachines.com leverages the digitized machinery and parts catalogs on the BigMachines.com Marketplace and also provides connections to other marketplaces and procurement platforms, such as Ariba and Commerce One. By working with industrial machinery sellers to define machinery-specific selection and configuration rules and build robust product catalogs, BigMachines.com provides machinery buyers with the most in-depth buying and collaboration tool.

BigMachines.com's original product focus was on fluid and rotating machinery, such as pumps, compressors, valves, and mixers, which are often components of an overall fluid system. Having built significant market share, the company is expanding to other machinery segments, such as power machinery (for example, motors) and fabrication equipment (for example, machine tools) and possibly to other types of complex products.

BigMachines.com is a global company operating in the United States; it also operates in Munich as BigMachines.com AG. The company expects to expand to Asia in 2001 and has already partnered with a major Japanese trading company.

ACHIEVING DOMINANCE

Within several months of its launch in May 2000, BigMachines.com has already signed on several leading global machinery manufacturers as clients. These customers include KSB AG, Europe's largest pump and valve manufacturer; ABEL Pumps, a wholly owned subsidiary of Roper Industries (NYSE: ROP); and two Fortune 500/Forbes Global 800 corporations. For these first customers, BigMachines. com is web-enabling product lines that represent several hundred million dollars in annual sales. The company has also partnered with top technology companies, such as webMethods, Ariba, Commerce One, and Idiom Technologies. The company has developed extensive relationships within the industrial sector through its industry advisory board and its financial backers. BigMachines.com's marketing programs include aggressive media relations activities, direct sales, speaking engagements, sponsorship of industry association events, and hosting of customer advisory workshops. The first BigMachines.com "E-Business for Engineered Systems Workshop," in July 2000, attracted 9 of the top 10 pump manufacturers in the world and executives from 40 top industrial corporations.

BUILDING A COMMUNITY—SERVICES ADDED TO THE TRADING MECHANISM

BigMachines.com has partnered with leading technology, content, and services providers to create a robust, feature-rich solution that is designed to support the dynamic growth of Internet-based B2B e-commerce. The company provides rapid, seamless integration to back-end enterprise resource planning (ERP) systems such as SAP, Baan, J.D. Edwards, Oracle, and PeopleSoft. The company has established alliances with Ariba and Commerce One to offer integration with buyer e-procurement systems. The BigMachines.com Marketplace provides industry-specific news, stock information, industry resource information, event calendars, and other information services. Through its partners, the company can also provide these services as part of its eSales solution to power a machinery seller's web site. The company is currently developing services to offer a logistics program for tracking and transportation of goods as well as electronic billing and credit options.

REVENUE MODEL

BigMachines.com revenues are based primarily on a combination of application service fees for use and hosting of the BigMachines.com Internet applications and transaction fees for sales generated through its Marketplace. BigMachines.com also receives professional service fees for the implementation of its Internet Sales Channel.

CONFIDENTIALITY AND NEUTRALITY

BigMachines.com is neutral; it does not own any of the products transacted through its Internet Sales Channel and Marketplace. BigMachines.com provides multiple forms of security, including encrypted communications and user ID/password, to ensure the appropriate levels of transaction security. The company is committed to fairness, confidentiality, and security.

For further information
BigMachines.com
558 Pilgrim Drive
Foster City, CA 94404
info@bigmachines.com

Catastrophe Risk Exchange (CATEX)

OVERVIEW

CATEX is the only impartial, global, Internet-based trading system for the insurance, reinsurance, and risk-bearing industry. A licensed reinsurance intermediary, CATEX brings insurers, reinsurers, brokers, self-insureds, and others together over the Internet to match buyers and sellers of risk and transact business. CATEX facilitates various risks, including environmental liability, marine, aviation, auto insurance, and others. CATEX enables primary insurers and reinsurers to more widely distribute their risks, as well as to diversify the perils they insure against.

HISTORY

CATEX was founded in August 1996 by Francis Fortunato, Francis Sweeney, and Samuel Fortunato. Late in 1996, CATEX launched a risk trading system that offered users direct-dial access to an ISDN-based private network using dedicated proprietary software. After

Internet technologies began to be adopted in the insurance industry, CATEX introduced a browser-based version of the trading system in November 1998. In December 1999, the company rolled out CATEX 2000, an Extensible Mark-up Language–based system developed by Tradeum. CATEX is a privately held company funded by investments from its founders, and from Science Applications International Corporation, E. W. Blanch, and Sculley Brothers LLC. The company has retained Lehman Brothers as its financial adviser and is currently engaged in a private placement.

VERTICAL MARKET OPPORTUNITY

CATEX was developed as a way to increase capacity for coverage against catastrophe. The trading system was well received by the industry and immediately brought greater efficiency and increased the amount of information available to buyers in the reinsurance industry. Since CATEX subscribers have all agreed to anonymously provide information about transactions completed on the system, CATEX is able to offer real-time posting of strike price, deal size, etc. when transactions are completed. Price transparency brings a host of benefits to the industry and fundamentally changes the way insurance and reinsurance risks are negotiated and transacted. CATEX, recognizing growing acceptance in the industry, now offers large corporate buyers of insurance the ability to check pricing on-line as well as a mechanism to buy directly.

MEMBERSHIP MODEL

CATEX is a privately held company controlled by its founders and a group of neutral commercial investors. Membership is open but is restricted to risk bearers, intermediaries, their subsidiaries and affiliates, and corporate risk managers. Representatives and firms applying for subscriptions are required to provide documentation confirming their legal status as a risk bearer or reinsurance intermediary.

TRADING MODEL

CATEX provides a flexible, secure environment for the negotiation of trades using an open "bid and ask" market, or exchange. The speed, efficiency, and flexibility of the CATEX Trading System enable subscribers to fashion innovative, integrated risk management strategies and packages. CATEX provides an ideal forum to enable electronic transactions involving cash premium payments, as well as pure risk swaps, and subscribers can use the trading system to sell or purchase traditional reinsurance products such as quota share, per-risk excess, or catastrophe excess coverage. CATEX also allows insurers and self-insured companies to purchase insurance and reinsurance directly from CATEX subscriber carriers. Risk bearers can diversify their potential liabilities by gaining access to wider risk distributions at minimal costs. Parties are able to respond to listings and negotiate trades by various methods, including CATEX e-mail, real-time text dialogue, on-line conferences, collaborative document processing, telephone, fax, or mail. The terms of an agreed trade can be finalized by traditional paper methods or by using the sophisticated on-line document management tools available in CATEX. Completed trades are registered with CATEX and their details publicized to all subscribers.

The company also has a patent pending on the CATEX Cross Domain Risk Management Trading System, which permits subscribing companies to use the CATEX technology under their own branding and control as subsystems of the global CATEX system. Switching easily between the domains and the global CATEX domain permits a company to use the CATEX award-winning technology privately and yet as part of the global system. The global CATEX subscriber membership exceeds two hundred companies.

Forbes.com included the CATEX site in its top two hundred B2B web sites in July 2000.

MARKET ENTRY STRATEGY

Before launching CATEX, the founders spent 18 months working with prospective customers to determine their needs and how best to design the proposed trading solution. Because the founders leveraged their expertise in the industry and focused on market needs before developing a technology platform, CATEX received widespread support from professionals who were willing to buy and sell reinsurance on the electronic exchange. Although CATEX initially focused on catastrophe reinsurance, 80% of postings on the trading system since startup have been for other types of insurance and reinsurance. CATEX not only has broadened its range of offerings to include additional lines of reinsurance and primary insurance, but also has enhanced its trading platform.

ACHIEVING DOMINANCE

CATEX is the world's largest electronic transaction system for the reinsurance and insurance industries. As of October 2000 CATEX had more than 2,500 postings and had completed more than 550 transactions representing approximately $3.2 billion in bound coverage and approximately $475 million in premiums. The site is open for trades 24 hours a day, seven days a week, and averages about eight thousand hits a day. All this activity is the result of participation by

204 subscribers and more than 2,200 users registered to trade on the exchange. About 50% of CATEX's subscribers are risk bearers and 20% are brokers. Another 30% are primary insurers and corporate risk managers, buyers of insurance and reinsurance whom CATEX plans to target more directly. In recent months the organization has focused its marketing message on the buyers, and this is the fastest growing subscriber group.

BUILDING A COMMUNITY—SERVICES ADDED TO THE TRADING MECHANISM

To provide an optimal analytical environment for informed risk trading, CATEX provides access to critical research tools as well as links to information sources such as insurance and financial news services, ratings and financial data for individual companies, catastrophe modeling packages, and other specialized risk management data sources. CATEX subscribers can access summary data on completed trades as well as on-line reports on special topics related to trading activities. The CATEX Document Center enables electronic distribution of entire underwriting submissions of information. CATEX offers subscribers the opportunity to set up a private CATEX network under their own brand. This allows customers to leverage the powerful CATEX trading platform in order to provide on-line insurance trading to their downstream customers and partners without investing large sums on development.

REVENUE MODEL

Subscription fees are CATEX's primary revenue source. Each participating firm pays an annual subscription fee to use CATEX trading facilities, as well as a trading commission of one-tenth of 1% (10 basis points) of the premium on sale of insurance or reinsurance on CATEX. Intermediary fees of 5% to 15% or 1,000 basis points are typical in the industry. CATEX does not charge for buyers' licenses for primary insurance companies and corporate risk managers. The buyers' license allows up to 10 users on the system. CATEX charges $2,000 per month for sellers' licenses for risk bearers and brokers. The sellers' license allows each member to have 50 employees trade on the exchange.

CONFIDENTIALITY AND NEUTRALITY

CATEX is a New York corporation that is licensed as a reinsurance intermediary acting in a neutral capacity by the New York Insurance Department. The company is subject to oversight and examination by the New York Superintendent of Insurance. CATEX users can use the trading system anonymously until a serious interest in trading is discovered. Following mutual disclosure of the identities of the transacting parties, negotiations proceed in a discreet fashion. CATEX has structured by-laws to ensure that no party may improperly obtain trading data, no sector of the insurance or reinsurance industry is unfairly affected or excluded, and the integrity and impartiality of CATEX are maintained at all times.

For further information
Francis Fortunato, CEO
CATEX, The Catastrophe Risk Exchange Inc.
26 Broadway, Suite 400
New York, NY 10004
1-877-GO-CATEX
francis_fortunato@catex.com

CreditTrade

OVERVIEW

CreditTrade is an Internet exchange designed to allow financial institutions to trade and manage credit risk. CreditTrade hopes to become the least expensive way to trade credit, costing nothing to use or access unless a trade is completed and negotiated through the site, when a commission will be charged. The credit derivatives marketplace is currently hindered by a lack of transparency and a shortage of standardized documentation. CreditTrade solves these problems by dramatically improving the ease, transparency, and efficiency with which institutions exchange documents and negotiate, trade, and manage credit risk. It also offers a comprehensive picture to all credit traders concentrating on credit derivatives, loan trading, and other structured credit trades. CreditTrade was initially funded by Mutant Technology.

HISTORY

London-based Mutant Technology was formed to exploit Internet technologies in the wholesale financial sector. The idea behind CreditTrade took hold in January 1999. Founded by Paul Ellis, CreditTrade was initially started and operated as part of Mutant Technology. CreditTrade.com was initially launched on a trial basis with simulated trading on 30 June 1999. The official launch with live trading was on 26 July 1999. It was formed as a separate company in September 1999.

VERTICAL MARKET OPPORTUNITY

In 1998, the British Bankers' Association estimated that the global credit derivatives market was $350 billion. This huge market was not being specifically targeted by any one party and was well understood by CreditTrade's founders. There is a crowded e-commerce marketplace for fixed income, bonds, and other commoditized retail products. The systems to deal with and settle these commodities are more easily understood and created. The credit marketplace is not commoditized; revenue depends on details of the trade that must be negotiated. For this reason it is less easily understood, and solutions are less easily implemented, which results in a less crowded marketplace.

There are two primary reasons why credit trading is well suited for the Internet: documentation and transparency. Because the web can be used to automate the occasionally extensive documentation required to define and close credit transactions, sharing between business partners can be streamlined. The CreditTrade web site provides a mechanism to upload, download, share, and forward documents involved in negotiating and closing a deal.

In addition, the web offers transparency, which is an improvement over the traditional system, in which brokers intermediate between different market players. Before the web introduced real-time communications, not everyone had access to all the information that might be available at any given time. Before CreditTrade, when trades were done, brokers had privileged information that became valuable when they talked to another market player. This presented problems of favoritism and decreased market liquidity; players who did not feel they were in the loop were less likely to take risks. The CreditTrade web site introduced an electronic broker that is efficient, transparent, and neutral. The most important thing the web does here is to bring transparency to the credit trading marketplace, with the goal of increasing volume.

MEMBERSHIP MODEL

CreditTrade is commercially owned with an open but qualified membership policy. All members are thoroughly evaluated before they can trade on CreditTrade. The compliance process includes verification of identity, as well as verification that users are members of a regulated institution in good standing. Because the financial markets are regulated in the United Kingdom by the SFA (an agency like the SEC in the United States), CreditTrade is looking to the stock markets for examples as its membership model continues to evolve.

TRADING MODEL

CreditTrade implements a post and browse system, giving users the ability to constrain what details can be viewed by other users. The post and browse system is enhanced and automated with the use of templates designed for different users. Deals are described and posted, and then users can search the CreditTrade database to find deals that match their needs.

If traders see a trade that interests them, they can correspond anonymously with the person who posted the trade. If they reach an agreement, CreditTrade will effect a simultaneous exchange of names (provided each party agrees to this), allowing completion of the trade directly. The parties then "lock" the deal on the system and clear credit or finalize the documentation off-line. Once a trade is executed, it must be reported back to the exchange. If the trade does not get executed off-line, the parties can "unlock" the trade on the system. Once a trade has been executed, that information is collated and published on the site to provide a price reference for other participants. CreditTrade is also expanding the trading system to provide a new "customer deals" area, where banks can provide deals directly to their customers via the CreditTrade site. The bank gives CreditTrade a list of people who are allowed to see various deals. CreditTrade does not charge the banks on a deal-by-deal basis, but charges a membership fee for the privilege of using the bulletin board.

MARKET ENTRY STRATEGY

CreditTrade gets in the middle of the deal flow; that is, it oils the engine of transactions. The market entry strategy was primarily to focus on the credit derivatives market as a subset of the larger and more crowded credit trading sector.

ACHIEVING DOMINANCE

CreditTrade has a growing base of traders. Marketers on staff at CreditTrade make on-site visits to encourage users to post trades and to help facilitate closing trades.

In February 2000, CreditTrade joined forces with Prebon Yamane, a leading global credit derivatives intermediary, to provide traders with greater access to real-time data, improved trading information, and enhanced liquidity via the Internet. Under the agreement, Prebon Yamane moved its global credit derivatives team (the bricks and mortar) and historical default swap database to CreditTrade in return for a substantial equity stake. In all, 13 credit derivatives brokers in London, New York, Singapore joined CreditTrade's on-line credit sales desk to form a single global team. The agreement highlights the potential benefits to all market users of combining the personal attention provided by traditional voice brokers with the speed, efficiency, and cost-effectiveness of an Internet B2B exchange.

In October 2000, CreditTrade celebrated its first anniversary by announcing that it has garnered a market share of around 40% of all interdealer trades worldwide. Regionally, it now has a 35% to 40% share in Europe, the United States, and Latin America and a 60% share in Asia.

BUILDING A COMMUNITY—SERVICES ADDED TO THE TRADING MECHANISM

In the past two and a half years, Mutant has developed a variety of technologies to power on-line trading systems. Much of this functionality has been incorporated into the CreditTrade exchange. In addition, CreditTrade uses Reuters News to provide credit industry news on the site and has a partnership with Market Abilities Unlimited to provide information and education about credit products, a resources section of the site, and forums for commentary about what is happening in the credit trading market.

REVENUE MODEL

CreditTrade's revenues will come from a combination of transaction commissions, membership fees, and subscription fees. If a trade gets done on the anonymous trading site as a result of a CreditTrade introduction, a commission based on the size of the deal is collected. CreditTrade would not specify the amount of the commission charged, but did indicate that it will almost always be less than a normal broker commission. In the customer area of the site, membership fees are charged for use of the bulletin board. These fees are based on overall trading volume, and no per-deal transaction commissions are charged. In certain cases, subscription fees are collected for access to market information generated by the trading mechanism.

CONFIDENTIALITY AND NEUTRALITY

All deals and communications on CreditTrade are anonymous. In addition, all data is encrypted, so traders can be confident that any information they send cannot be intercepted. Although anyone can get a password to access the site, "trader" status is required to view, post, and respond to trades. Neutrality is ensured because the exchange is widely held by an investment group.

For further information
CreditTrade
12/13 Henrietta Street
London, WC2E 8LH
United Kingdom
paule@mutant-tech.com

e-Chemicals, Inc.

OVERVIEW

e-Chemicals is a provider of e-supply chain solutions for the chemical industry. e-Chemicals is the first Internet-based company dedicated to offering an optimized e-supply chain management solution that improves transaction efficiency, enhances e-supply chain management with trading partners, and allows optimal connectivity for greater data visibility and improved business processes. By developing solutions that link raw materials providers, chemical manufacturers, channel intermediaries, and chemical purchasers, e-Chemicals drives significant value by creating efficiencies and reducing costs through best-of-breed technology and a premium solution set.

HISTORY

e-Chemicals was founded in 1998 by Alf Sherk, Lorne Darnell, and Yossi Sheffi. The site was launched in July 1998. Headquartered in Addison, Texas, e-Chemicals is owned by its founders, employees, and holding company, Internet Capital Group (Nasdaq: ICGE). e-Chemicals has been generating revenue for a year and is focused on market dominance. Because of this, the company is continually investing in expanding their offerings and acquiring customers.

VERTICAL MARKET OPPORTUNITY

e-Chemicals was established to address the challenges facing the chemical industry: inefficient and complex supply chains, interdependent and interconnected participants, and the strong customer demand for e-business solutions. Solving this challenge of the fragmented chemical supply market is the driving principle behind e-Chemicals. The e-Chemicals management team has more than 150 years of collective experience in chemical logistics, manufacturing, and distribution. The company relies on this industry expertise and insight into the supply chain challenges of the chemicals industry to deliver integrated solutions for the industry. e-Chemicals first concentrated on on-line commerce, enabling customers to facilitate a purchase from order to delivery through one transaction. The company then enhanced its services by developing an optimized e-supply chain solution that goes beyond simple Internet-enabled transactions.

MEMBERSHIP MODEL

e-Chemicals is a privately held company. Customers are prequalified buyers and suppliers of industrial chemicals.

TRADING MODEL

e-Chemicals launched its web site with a multivendor catalog. Today, the company improves transaction efficiency by reducing logistics and procurement and sales expenses; enhancing e-supply chains for plant optimization, inventory reductions, and process efficiency; and optimizing connectivity to provide customers greater data visibility and improved business processes.

MARKET ENTRY STRATEGY

e-Chemicals focuses is exclusively on the industrial chemical segment. The company's first priority was to develop an integrated, online business model that enables it to serve as a neutral channel for both the supplier and the customer in executing the secure and rapid procurement, sale, and distribution of industrial chemicals.

e-Chemicals believes that e-commerce will be an integrated component of a multichannel distribution process and has designed its service to adapt to the needs of individual procurement professionals. In 2000, e-Chemicals expanded its offering to include e-procurement solutions for large corporate chemical buyers. Specifically, e-Chemicals works with the purchasing organizations to streamline the procurement process by eliminating as many steps as possible and automating the rest. The next step is to focus on strategic sourcing initiatives, such as aggregation of demand and implementation of dynamic pricing tools. e-Chemicals' ultimate goal is the integration of its e-commerce system with its customers' ERP and other legacy systems.

ACHIEVING DOMINANCE

As of October 1999, e-Chemicals had more than 1,000 products listed on its site, 600 registered buyers, as well as 20 manufacturers and suppliers. e-Chemicals markets itself aggressively through a variety of marketing and sales strategies. Ads placed in chemical trade publications focus on brand awareness. The company's public relations efforts include media relations, industry analyst relations, and the executive speaking circuit. e-Chemicals has a dedicated direct-sales force to sell its e-supply chain solutions to large customers. e-Chemicals has alliances with more than 25 of the top chemical industry suppliers and distributors. In addition, it has partnerships with world-class market leaders, including webMethods, CommerceQuest, SunTrust, Yellow Services, and Aspen Technologies.

BUILDING A COMMUNITY—SERVICES ADDED TO THE TRADING MECHANISM

e-Chemicals provides daily industry news and feature reports on critical issues that affect the chemicals market and e-commerce industry. A feedback mechanism on the site permits customers to submit questions, and a customer service call-in number is posted on the site. e-Chemicals has added the AMS ProSteward system for document management and compliance reporting to meet environmental, health, and service regulations.

REVENUE MODEL

e-Chemicals' revenue model is based on a philosophy of shared and created value with customers.

CONFIDENTIALITY AND NEUTRALITY

e-Chemicals is a neutral partner. In addition, access to e-Chemicals' high-security web site is limited by user name and password, and all customer registration information and order data are encrypted for secure transactions. This security, coupled with the company's published confidentiality policy, assures customers that their data will not be misused.

For further information
e-Chemicals
4450 Sojourn Drive, Suite 100
Addison, TX
1-734-827-3411
info@e-chemicals.com

e-STEEL

OVERVIEW

e-STEEL Corporation is the leading provider of open e-commerce solutions that strategically connect the global metals supply chain and solve complex business problems to create real value. Through its Internet-based B2B public marketplace, e-STEEL enables thousands of companies worldwide to purchase and sell prime and non-prime products, including hot rolled, cold rolled, coated, sheet, plate, tin mill, rebar, semifinished slabs, and wire rod. e-STEEL plans to add pipe and tube, structural, and other metals over the next few months. Its advanced, negotiation-based e-commerce exchange provides the metals industry with a robust, secure on-line marketplace that also features rich, up-to-date industry information and community resources. e-STEEL was the first metal industry exchange to offer complete end-to-end system integration through its e-STEEL CONNECT[sm] hub-and-spoke technology, which uses Steel Mark-up Language, an extension of Extensible Mark-up Language that e-STEEL initiated and then helped global industry standards committees define and develop.

e-STEEL is more than a marketplace. This year, e-STEEL expanded its leadership and revenue structure to include more than exchange transaction fees. The company developed several domain solution provider (DSPs) applications, such as private marketplaces and collaborative value chain solutions that automate several complex business problems through the Internet. The company also derives revenue from consulting, value-added services, and advertising.

In its first year, e-STEEL secured committed strategic alliances with top industry leaders, such as Ford Motor Company, U.S. Steel Group, Ispat International, Dofasco Inc. National Steel, Rouge Steel, Macsteel Service Centers USA, USS-Posco, Worthington Steel, The Techs, and BHP. It also signed a memorandum of understanding to develop and power a European regional marketplace with four prominent steel companies and became a partner in the leading Japanese domestic marketplace joint venture, SMART Online.

e-STEEL is well funded, having raised more than $100 million from a blue-chip group of strategic investors led by Goldman Sachs and including Amerindo Investment Advisors; Bessemer Venture Partners; Dofasco Inc.; DuPont; GE Capital; Generation Partners; Greylock; Ispat International; Kleiner Perkins Caufield & Byers; Mitsui & Company U.S.A.; Mitsubishi International and MC Capital Inc., subsidiaries of Mitsubishi Corp.; U.S. Steel; and Vulcan Ventures.

e-STEEL has offices in New York, Pittsburgh, Chicago, Bethesda, Detroit, Atlanta, Brussels, Singapore, and Sydney.

HISTORY

For almost a decade, Michael S. Levin, e-STEEL's founder, CEO, and chairman, envisioned setting up a 24-hour international electronic marketplace to buy and sell steel. He recognized that the Internet presented a solution to many of the business problems that plagued the metals industry and founded e-STEEL in September 1998. After spending months developing the proper business model, e-STEEL became one of the first B2B exchanges in any industry and chose Computer Sciences Corporation (CSC) as a technology partner and began site development. In the spring of 1999, e-STEEL began testing and simulated trading. It began accepting new membership applications at the end of July 1999. The first trade, involving prime hot rolled steel, was closed between Cargill and Worthington Industries shortly after the formal launch of the e-STEEL exchange in September 1999. Since then, e-STEEL has undergone tremendous enhancements and expansion of its e-commerce technologies through its strong, domain-specific, in-house engineering group.

In 2000, major industry leaders including Ford Motor Company, U.S. Steel, Ispat International, Dofasco Inc. National Steel, Rouge Steel, Macsteel Service Centers USA, USS-Posco, Worthington Steel, The Techs, and BHP selected e-STEEL as their e-commerce alliance provider. In addition, nearly five thousand other companies, representing all the key segments of the steel value chain, are members of e-STEEL.

e-STEEL also expanded its revenue structure and leadership in 2000 by developing several DSP applications. These include private marketplaces and collaborative value chain solutions that e-enable several complex business problems.

VERTICAL MARKET OPPORTUNITY

Although steel is a $700 billion global industry and one of the largest industries worldwide, it has no central marketplace. The fragmented market makes it difficult for buyers and sellers to find each other.

Phones, faxes, and paper-intensive documentation created high, labor-intensive transaction costs. The industry lacks transparency and faces tremendous profitability challenges. Steel industry leaders believed that e-commerce is a way to streamline purchases and better serve their customers, yet there was no clarity regarding how and when e-commerce solutions would be adopted.

After working in several segments of the steel industry for more than 25 years, Michael S. Levin had access to CEOs and other decision makers and began to gather information from them to determine what type of solution was needed. Relying on his industry experience, Levin gained early participation by companies willing to invest the time to find out whether e-STEEL's solution worked for them. Through this early collaborative testing and evaluation process, Levin learned what e-STEEL needed to do, was able to see what worked, and determined what additional features were needed.

MEMBERSHIP MODEL

e-STEEL is a neutral marketplace owned by a strategic group of blue-chip investors. Its board of directors has no ties to or involvement with any steel industry participants. To become an e-STEEL member, companies must be legitimate buyers or suppliers of steel products and must pass a qualification process, which includes a credit check and corporate profile.

TRADING MODEL

The e-STEEL exchange operates on a negotiation basis between buyer and seller and can be initiated by either side. The foundation of the exchange is a proprietary combination of electronic commerce and personalization software that enables users to easily search product availability or RFQs, post orders or RFQs, and complete online negotiations to buy and sell steel. For example, a buyer could make an offer on a selected product, and the seller could award it or make a counteroffer. The buyer could accept the counteroffer or make another offer. Sellers may list products for sale directly over e-STEEL. Sales contracts between the buyers and sellers continue to regulate transactions. All transactions are fully documented on the e-STEEL system, and e-STEEL monitors compliance with exchange rules. The site also features a proprietary, advanced, customization application called STEELDIRECT™, which is a system that enables targeted, private on-line channel and customer/supplier relationship management.

MARKET ENTRY STRATEGY

The metals industry is pyramidal, with about two hundred large companies producing seven hundred tons of product per year for an estimated 1 million end users worldwide. e-STEEL targets the large steel producers, all the subsequent buyers and sellers of steel in the complex value chain, as well as large original equipment manufacturer (OEM) buyers (such as automotive and appliance manufacturers) as it builds traction. By providing services to both suppliers and buyers, e-STEEL hopes to become the industry standard that can facilitate the most cost-efficient transactions and e-enable complex business processes for all segments of the global metal supply chain.

ACHIEVING DOMINANCE

Currently, e-STEEL serves nearly five thousand member companies from a hundred countries representing all the key segments of the value chain: mills, service centers, fabricators, converters, international trading companies, and OEM/end users. E-commerce in the metals industry gained significant momentum in 2000, but it has not yet gained critical mass. Analysts predict that within the next four years about 40% to 60% of all steel transactions will involve the Internet and exchanges like e-STEEL. e-STEEL's expansion to "more than a marketplace" via its DSP applications (for example, private marketplaces and e-enabled collaborative value chain solutions) will likely enable it to provide similar solutions for other highly attributed metals and raw materials in the next few months. The breadth of its technology leadership, its deep domain knowledge and industry experience, and the strength of its executive management team are e-STEEL's competitive advantages.

BUILDING A COMMUNITY—SERVICES ADDED TO THE TRADING MECHANISM

e-STEEL also provides industry news, calendars, tools and resources, job listings, weather, and stock data. It is working with several technology partners, such as webMethods, to further deliver supply chain and purchasing system integration solutions. e-STEEL is developing systems that in the future will allow buyers to negotiate credit terms on-line and authorize e-STEEL to pay the seller. In addition, once a transaction is negotiated, buyers will be able to connect with e-STEEL logistics partners to arrange delivery. Because on e-STEEL information on a user's searches, purchases, and channel management company is easily archived, the transaction processes become significantly more streamlined, which saves tremendous time and makes the e-STEEL solution more valuable the more it is used.

REVENUE MODEL

e-STEEL derives revenue from several sources. It charges sellers an exchange transaction fee (on a sliding scale, based on committed volume) of less than 1% on all purchases concluded on the site. e-STEEL also receives revenue from annual technology subscription fees, consulting, value-added services, and advertising.

CONFIDENTIALITY AND NEUTRALITY

e-STEEL is an independent, neutral e-commerce solution provider. No industry participant sits on its board of directors. It does not own or take title to any of the products transacted on the system. All information is kept in the strictest confidence, and all participants are treated fairly in order to guarantee high satisfaction levels, as well as to encourage trading activity.

For further information
e-STEEL Corporation
1250 Broadway, 30th Floor
New York, NY 10022
1-212-527-9997
info@e-STEEL.com

MetalSite

OVERVIEW

MetalSite is a neutral, secure Internet marketplace for buying and selling metals products. It also serves as a comprehensive industry resource for news and information. For metals buyers, MetalSite is a comprehensive resource for up-to-date information about their industry and the products being offered by manufacturers. For sellers, MetalSite presents an opportunity to expand their customer base, increase efficiencies in the selling process, turn over inventory more quickly, and free up the sales force from non-value-added tasks. MetalSite has recently transitioned aggressively into phase 2 of its business plan by developing solutions that will improve the metals supply chain. Services such as supply chain collaborative planning, order status, order management, and back office integration will dramatically help metals companies achieve supply chain visibility and drive down excess inventories.

HISTORY

MetalSite was initiated in 1996, when founder and CEO Patrick Stewart was asked to develop an Internet strategy for his employer, Weirton Steel Corporation, the eighth largest steel producer in the United States. Stewart and his team of experts recognized the tremendous inefficiencies that existed along the entire metals supply chain and saw the Internet as a cost-effective solution to these inefficiencies. Using Weirton Steel as a test site and proving ground for the concept of buying and selling steel products on-line, Stewart made an initial investment of $3 million to conduct extensive research and testing, before launching the MetalSite marketplace in 1998. MetalSite is a privately held limited partnership. Initial investors included industry participants LTV Steel, Steel Dynamics, and Weirton Steel. In September 1999, industry giants Bethlehem Steel and Ryerson Tull joined as new investors. MetalSite's current investors represent nearly 22% of steel shipped in the United States annually. MetalSite expects to be "cash neutral" by the end of its second year of operation.

VERTICAL MARKET OPPORTUNITY

Although the world's metals industry produces 750 million tons per year, the largest U.S. producer claims only a 10% market share. Patrick Stewart is a steel industry veteran who saw an opportunity to streamline the inefficient and fragmented metals supply chain. He recognized that the Internet provides a real-time communications network that can centralize and streamline the inefficient and complex network of buyers.

The MetalSite think-tank reviewed thousands of pages of information about the Internet, e-commerce, and the steel industry and then conducted customer interviews and surveys to gather information on how the web site should be structured. This research was supplemented by discussions with experts, including Thomas Malone, a professor at the Massachusetts Institute of Technology and an early theorist on the impact of electronic marketplaces; Mark Teflian, creator of the Apollo airline reservation system and current chief technology officer for Perot Systems and the Doblin Group, a world leader in creating user-driven strategy concepts. The research, especially that conducted by the Doblin Group, focused on steel buyers' behavior and helped determine how the marketplace should be designed as well as how MetalSite could be effectively marketed.

MEMBERSHIP MODEL

MetalSite is a privately owned corporation composed of industry participants. Although initially funded in part by the steel industry's largest producers, MetalSite offers open membership and has gone to great lengths to provide a neutral marketplace and ensure that customers' information is kept strictly confidential. Visitors must complete a buyer's profile before they may enter the on-line marketplace. MetalSite verifies the legitimacy of the buyers, and creditworthiness is determined by the seller.

TRADING MODEL

The MetalSite marketplace offers a wide range of options for buying and selling prime and nonprime products and provides a single point where users can easily and cost-effectively locate and purchase products from multiple companies on-line. The MetalSite catalog includes a product guide and sealed-bid auction. The product guide supports a price list, contract pricing, volume discount pricing and on-line negotiations. Prime and nonprime products are offered in an auction format, with traditional channels used for payment and logistics. Sellers can solicit bids, privately review them, and then award the sale. Bid solicitation, submission, and award are all conducted privately via MetalSite. In September 2000, MetalSite introduced a highly advanced RFQ system call QuoteFinder. The design of QuoteFinder is based on industry knowledge and customer feedback and is seen today as one of the most advanced and easy-to-use RFQ systems on the Internet. By the second quarter of 2001, MetalSite will introduce contract order management capabilities to support high volumes of prime product sales.

MARKET ENTRY STRATEGY

To build a successful marketplace that would attract buyers, MetalSite initially secured commitments from major steel producers to commit inventory on a daily basis and list a substantial volume of product for sale monthly. These steel suppliers were leaders and innovators in the national and international marketplaces and brought both credibility and product to the MetalSite marketplace. MetalSite continues to recruit new sellers to ensure that buyers will participate in trading.

MetalSite built its web marketplace in strategic phases, launching with content and community services and then adding e-commerce capabilities. Initially, MetalSite offered excess prime and secondary products via a low-risk, sealed-bid auction for buyers and sellers. Later, products and services were expanded to include prime and made-to-order products in a catalog format supporting a list price, contract pricing, volume discount pricing, and on-line negotiations. Services such as banking, logistics, and on-line order status were added, and electronic purchase orders, bill collection, and bill payment systems were also introduced. The next phase of implementation will expand product offerings to include metals such as aluminium, copper, and zinc and will make available unparalleled industry reports created from the purchasing data generated by the electronic marketplace.

ACHIEVING DOMINANCE

MetalSite currently has more than 3,000 active buying companies and more than 24,000 registered associates. It has grown from three initial sellers to a projected one hundred by the end of 2000. Monthly product volume has grown from 20,000 tons to more than 120,000 tons, representing more than $45 million worth of product available for sale at the MetalSite marketplace on a monthly basis. MetalSite's marketing programs include print and on-line trade advertising, aggressive media relations activities, one-on-one sales, participation in and sponsorship of industry events, as well as speaking engagements.

BUILDING A COMMUNITY—SERVICES ADDED TO THE TRADING MECHANISM

The MetalSite marketplace delivers all the services required to research an order, find a product, and make a selection; to order and track a product, and to pay and settle the order. Other services Metal-Site plans to implement by early 2001 include banking services such as electronic billing and credit options; accounting services such as on-line order status and an electronic purchase order system; and a logistics program that offers a range of tracking and transportation features and more advanced supply chain solutions.

REVENUE MODEL

Buyers can access and use the site for free. Sellers are charged a transaction fee ranging from .25% up to 2% of each on-line sale. In addition, MetalSite offers consulting services for the development of an individual market center that basically is a mini web site for vendors that want to be represented on the MetalSite marketplace. Advertising sponsorships and banners are also available. With the new collaborative planning, order status, and integration services, MetalSite will introduce service fees on a pay-for-use basis.

CONFIDENTIALITY AND NEUTRALITY

Security and confidentiality are extremely important issues at MetalSite. The Arthur Andersen Risk Management Group audits MetalSite's business practices, policies, and procedures every six months. A copy of the audit and the MetalSite business practices are published on the MetalSite homepage for access by all visitors. MetalSite also requires that all employees sign a confidentiality agreement that legally binds them to comply with the company's strict rules of confidentiality and business practices as a condition of employment.

For further information
MetalSite, Inc.
Penn Center West
Building Two, Suite 200
Pittsburgh, PA 15276
1-877-246-4900
1-412-490-4900
info@metalsite.net

NTE (formerly the National Transportation Exchange)

OVERVIEW

NTE, formerly known as the National Transportation Exchange (NTE), is an electronic transportation marketplace that uses Internet technology to provide shippers, third-party logistics companies, and motor carriers with a trusted electronic network that eliminates supply chain inefficiencies and improves the productivity and profit margins of its members. NTE connects shippers who have loads they want to move efficiently with fleet managers who have space to fill. It offers real-time transportation procurement services and information management tools that help shippers and carriers in the United States leverage people and resources to make better transportation decisions.

HISTORY

Gregory Rocque conceived of NTE in 1993 and launched it in 1994. Its first trade occurred in March 1995, and the first web-based interface was introduced in December 1997. NTE is backed by an estimated $71 million in funding from AT&T Ventures, Hummer Winblad Venture Partners, Crosspoint Venture Partners, Generation Partners, FedEx, Bessemer Venture Partners, and Platinum Venture Partners. The company is not yet profitable. In 2000, *Red Herring* named NTE "one of the 100 most important companies in the world" and *Forbes* ranked it "one of the top 20 logistics and transportation B2B companies."

VERTICAL MARKET OPPORTUNITY

For years, trucking companies and shippers have been trying to coordinate loads with empty trucks, yet the complex web of trucking routes and the often random needs of companies that ship products have presented problems that are difficult to solve. As a result, many truckers leave drop-off points without full loads rather than go through the hassle of trying to find shippers whose needs match their return routes. Similarly, many trucks return from their destinations empty. Logistics industry experts estimate that in the motor carrier industry alone, capacity may be underused by as much as 50% today. This underuse is costing buyers and sellers of transportation services billions of dollars annually. NTE aims to reduce some of this inefficiency in distribution and transaction costs from the $400 billion trucking business.

Although "freight matching" services tried to address these problems, the lack of a real-time communications medium and incompatible information technology deployment prevented the development of an effective mechanism to link shippers and carriers. NTE's executive team recognized that widespread adoption of Internet and e-commerce technologies would create a virtually seamless shipping environment that could allow supply executives to manage the logistics of information as effectively as they manage the logistics of their inventory. NTE delivers a solution to the complicated problems of the transportation business, improving supply chain performance by enabling reliable, real-time visibility for the execution of transportation transactions.

MEMBERSHIP MODEL

NTE is neutrally owned by commercial investors and has open, qualified membership policies. NTE screens trucking companies to ensure that only reputable and insured companies are listed. To trade, members are qualified on the basis of safety ratings, insurance, size of fleet, type of freight, and credit history. Shippers are screened to ensure proper credit ratings. They join NTE after agreeing to membership rules that specify the type of freight than can be transported and their handling requirements, such as prompt load and unload times. Its prequalified membership program assures a vibrant marketplace for reputable trading partners. NTE ensures the quality, integrity, and settlement of every transaction. Membership in NTE's trading exchange is free.

TRADING MODEL

NTE collects shipment orders in its database, computes a market price for each one, and then matches them to truck routes provided by carriers. The database is updated instantly as new shipments are tendered, and carriers can get a list of loads that meet their route plans in seconds. NTE's system allows members to interactively match desirable rates for shipments by quoting a confirmed price for approval before it is committed by the shipper, or accepted by the carrier, in the electronic marketplace. When the delivery of the shipment is confirmed, NTE pays the carrier and invoices the shipper.

NTE creates a spot market by setting daily prices based on the trading activities of several hundred fleet managers about the destinations of their vehicles and the amount of space available. It then aligns the compatible deals. NTE's pricing models use custom software to factor in the shipping route, time, date, temperature, and distance. NTE tells carriers how much profit they stand to make with each load, which takes away the uncertainty that often deters truckers from taking on more cargo. NTE has defined processes, data capture and reporting, interfaces to related technologies, and even provides transportation billing and payment with third-party oversight.

MARKET ENTRY STRATEGY

Initially, NTE focused on the key players in a small region. After proving the business model and demonstrating the security and reliability of the trading engine, NTE began to expand its services and membership. Since its formation, NTE has developed a robust technology infrastructure designed to meet the specific needs of the transportation industry—a system that now serves the entire country and would not be easily replicated.

ACHIEVING DOMINANCE

Currently, NTE has more than six hundred members. NTE's carrier membership includes contract carrier fleets, dedicated carrier fleets, and the private fleets of major corporations. Shipper membership includes all segments of manufacturing, retailers, third-party logistics companies, and distributors. NTE continues to grow its membership using a variety of on-line and off-line marketing and sales activities. The company is focusing on building a customer base large enough to attract even more business and liquidity, or high trading volume.

BUILDING A COMMUNITY—SERVICES ADDED TO THE TRADING MECHANISM

NTE continues to develop new functionality with a focus on navigability, reliability, and scalability as features are added to enhance both the e-commerce system and supply chain integration. This includes Internet and Extranet tools for members. NTE's goal is to provide tight integration between the back-end systems of suppliers and buyers. To provide increased connectivity and integration between motor carriers and shippers, NTE has software alliances with companies such as SAP AG, Manugistics, i2 Technologies, McLeod Software, TMW Systems, and Creative Systems. To open new distribution channels, the company also has developed alliances with other logistics companies, such as FreightWise, RightFreight, and TruckersB2B.com. NTE aims to provide members with a wide range of information to maximize their business, all accessible from one point.

REVENUE MODEL

NTE collects a variable margin on each transaction. It represents the difference between what the shipper pays and the carrier receives. When a deal is agreed, NTE issues the contract and handles payment.

CONFIDENTIALITY AND NEUTRALITY

NTE is a neutral marketplace. Member confidentiality is preserved until a transaction is created, at which time the identities of both parties are revealed.

For further information
NTE
1400 Opus Place, Suite 650
Downers Grove, IL 60515
info@nte.com

PaperExchange

OVERVIEW

PaperExchange is an Internet marketplace for paper buyers, sellers, traders, and brokers. All grades of paper, from first quality to trim rolls, can be bought or sold on the exchange. With members in 75 countries and 24-hour site access seven days a week, the Paper-Exchange trading floor provides the most efficient worldwide marketplace for paper. PaperExchange is a global neutral marketplace. Members own, sell, and buy the paper; set prices; and establish terms for transfer. All paper is bought and sold through secured, anonymous transactions. PaperExchange does not share its list of members or its transaction information.

HISTORY

Hilton Plein founded PaperExchange's predecessor company in late 1996. Initially, the company's focus was in the containerboard arena only, and the real expansion of PaperExchange into all major paper grades happened after the current investors became involved in 1998. PaperExchange has remained focused on developing the exchange as the core of the business, with additional services to offer more value to members. The primary investors are the Kraft Group (the major investor to date), Internet Capital Group (approximately 25%), Terrapin Partners, and Roger Stone (former CEO of Stone Container Corp). Internet Capital Group became investor/owners in August 1999, and additional funding was received from all investors in September 1999. PaperExchange is headquartered in Boston, Massachusetts. The company is not yet profitable and is currently focused on building leadership and market share.

VERTICAL MARKET OPPORTUNITY

Extensive industry expertise is one of PaperExchange's major strengths. The founders have experience in the containerboard industry, and the company has recruited industry professionals across all major paper grades. Key managers in sales, business development, marketing, and information technology all come from within the pulp and paper industry and ensure that PaperExchange delivers the tools its users need.

Paper manufacturers still rely on a complex network of distributors, brokers, and reps. The result is market inefficiency and chronic imbalances between supply and demand. The founders of PaperExchange identified a large market that could benefit from an exchange system. PaperExchange more efficiently matches buyers with sellers, which is important in a volatile market with inconsistent demand. Because paper is a global business, it is subject to the many different demand cycles throughout the regional and national economies. With no current exchange-based hedging tools available, market players are exposed to influences that no single player can control.

This situation is complicated by the fact that traditional pricing instruments are often late and not representative of the actual transactions taking place at any given time. PaperExchange plans to deliver a solution to these problems and may bring the paper industry its first real-time public pricing forum. If successful, PaperExchange could smooth supply and demand fluctuations and perhaps even offer risk management tools.

MEMBERSHIP MODEL

PaperExchange is owned by commercial investors and has open membership. The site is neutral and independent and operates autonomously from any other pulp and paper organization or company. Membership of the exchange is available to all pulp and paper and related industry professionals. Although only members may buy or sell on the exchange, visitors may use the service for informational purposes.

TRADING MODEL

PaperExchange operates a true exchange with real-time pricing and on-line trade execution. The company provides a proactive matching service between buyers and sellers of paper and pulp products and related services. PaperExchange provides a bidding system that enables buyers to bid on products offered by a seller, or buyers can list requests to purchase products. PaperExchange also offers a "clearing" process and will guarantee payments by certain buyers whose creditworthiness has been approved.

MARKET ENTRY STRATEGY

PaperExchange initially targeted sellers to gain critical mass and increase paper volume on the exchange. After gaining acceptance and participation from a large number of suppliers/manufacturers who provided product to the site, PaperExchange is now working to expand its buyer membership. PaperExchange's original product focus was on containerboard, one of the larger sectors in the pulp and paper industry. After gaining market share in this area, the company expanded to include other paper grades. Currently, the major focus is on expanding on-line offerings to include printing and writing papers. The company is also enhancing features and services available on the site.

ACHIEVING DOMINANCE

In October 1999, PaperExchange had more than two thousand corporate members. The exchange is used by several hundred paper buyers and sellers in 75 countries, including nine of the top dozen suppliers in the United States. To drive business in the $300 billion annual world paper market, PaperExchange relies on a variety of sales and marketing activities, including public relations, trade shows, and trade and on-line advertising.

BUILDING A COMMUNITY—SERVICES ADDED TO THE TRADING MECHANISM

The PaperExchange web site provides news, stock information, industry resource information, event calendars, equipment sales, and career and other information services. PaperExchange delivers clearing and logistics services via international partners. Credit services, back-office systems, and direct links from users' systems directly to PaperExchange will be introduced shortly.

REVENUE MODEL

PaperExchange's primary revenues are derived from a 3% transaction fee charged to suppliers for each purchase made using the service. There are no membership fees or charges for posting products for sale.

CONFIDENTIALITY AND NEUTRALITY

PaperExchange is a neutral marketplace with a commitment to fairness, confidentiality, and security. PaperExchange controls access and use of the service through a combination of a customer ID, employee ID, and password. The exchange allows members to post anonymously and makes every attempt to preserve the anonymity of the parties and credit ratings until a transaction is agreed on. At that time, buyer and seller identities and credit ratings are revealed so that logistics and payment terms can be finalized. PaperExchange expects to be the first in the on-line paper industry to pass the stringent guidelines set for data security and privacy when it gains certification from Ernst & Young on security of data.

For further information
PaperExchange
545 Boylston Street, 8th Floor
Boston, MA 02116
1-617-536-4310
info@paperexchange.com

TechEx

OVERVIEW

TechEx is the leading Internet exchange for technology transfer in the life science industry. TechEx facilitates targeted communications between technology transfer offices at research institutions and corporate technology developers. The TechEx web site automatically links technology and intellectual property listings from leading research organizations and emerging bioscience companies to licensing executives in major life science companies. Members can scan new technology opportunities efficiently, without the distraction of inappropriate and unwanted information. Simultaneously, the network helps technology providers target interested commercial developers. TechEx is not yet profitable and recently completed first-round funding.

HISTORY

Originally created by Jon Garen at the Yale University Office of Cooperative Research in 1997, a patent application for TechEx, as a way to leverage the Internet as a medium for technology transfer, was filed in 1998. Perceived to have significant commercial value by Yale University, TechEx was licensed exclusively to Intellectual Property Technology Exchange, Inc. in June 1999. Spinning TechEx out as a separate, for-profit company not only provides the capital necessary for aggressive growth, but also positions the company to take advantage of commercial opportunities that were not the focus of a nonprofit university. Sculley Brothers LLC is an investor in TechEx.

VERTICAL MARKET OPPORTUNITY

Garen and Yale University recognized that getting technology out of an academic institution is slow going unless researchers have a strong relationship with their institution's technology transfer office and the case manager in that office has established contacts with potential buyers of the technology. Garen believed that the Internet could solve some of these relationship issues by better targeting technologies to the people who need them. The TechEx exchange was launched to serve the needs of the life science industry, which represents 70% of the early-stage technology transfer market. TechEx already has a strong hold on the academic institutions that spend more than $800 million annually to license life science technology. The company is focused on developing value-added services as it seeks to gain critical mass in the almost $6 billion annual world market for technology transfer in the life science industry (including related merger and acquisition activity). Only after reaching critical mass in life sciences does TechEx plan to expand into other verticals by superimposing their model into the information technology and physical sciences markets.

MEMBERSHIP MODEL

TechEx is owned by commercial investors and has open, qualified membership. Participation is restricted to technology transfer officers from accredited research institutions, corporate licensing professionals capable of bringing early-stage inventions to market, and credible investors capable of providing financial assistance to commercialization efforts. TechEx is diligent about confirming the institutional or corporate affiliation of members as well as authenticating that the person in the organization has the authority to buy or sell technology. Access to the TechEx service is secure and protected by the use of passwords; casual users are not permitted to use the system.

TRADING MODEL

TechEx implements a post and browse trading model with automated, anonymous e-mail communication and push e-mail notification. TechEx's initial offering, the DiscoveryExchange™, allows registered researchers to describe the technologies they want to sell, while allowing company managers to create "interest profiles" describing the kinds of research they want to track. Once a technology is posted, the system uses a keyword and semantic search function to match technology descriptions to the defined interests of potential buyers. Once a match occurs, TechEx notifies both parties electronically, providing a link back to their account on the system. The DiscoveryExchange also offers contextual information about the featured technology, such as market intelligence, intellectual property intelligence (patents), and research intelligence, which enables the recipients to better evaluate the licensing opportunity.

By pushing technology directly to appropriate recipients, based on their own self-described interests, and returning a recipient list to universities, TechEx will replace current marketing practices with a more efficient approach. Trading and clearing functions are currently in development with a strategic partner and will be deployed once TechEx begins charging transaction fees.

MARKET ENTRY STRATEGY

Launched by Yale, TechEx initially targeted research institutions with a solution to facilitate academic technology transfer activities. The university platform was particularly beneficial for TechEx, since not-for-profit organizations frequently have access to technology earlier than corporations, and because more and more corporations are out-sourcing research to universities. In fact, the research institution holds enormous credibility in the life science vertical. This is due primarily to strong academic and medical ties that are not as prevalent in other technology transfer markets, such as information technology and physical science. With a strong offering for research institutions now in place and widely embraced, TechEx has a critical mass of institutional users and is more likely to be able to attract corporate participation. After the technology platform is fully developed, TechEx plans to expand into other technology transfer markets. Recently, TechEx has broadened corporate participation to facilitate corporate-to-corporate technology exchange on the DiscoveryExchange.

ACHIEVING DOMINANCE

With more than 500 corporate organizations registered, including biotechnology, pharmaceutical, and investment companies, and more than 250 world-renowned research organizations, TechEx boasts an average of 25 technologies listed weekly and has 3,200 technologies currently listed in the database. To date, more than 120,000 connections have taken place between research scientists and licensing professionals. The TechEx web site now tracks about half of the 50 to 60 new life science technologies developed weekly across the country. A strong customer service program ensures that existing members will make the transition as TechEx begins charging membership fees. To grow rapidly, TechEx has outsourced all technology development and relies on strategic partnerships to drive content offerings and attract new users. Traditional marketing in on-line and off-line media is being used to attract new members and educate existing members about new services.

BUILDING A COMMUNITY—SERVICES ADDED TO THE TRADING MECHANISM

In conjunction with respected strategic partners, TechEx plans to provide critical informational content around its listings to allow buyers to more accurately and quickly make decisions about whether to pursue a technology. Some features in development include providing members with instant access to related research, information about competitive technologies, and background information on both inventors and their institutions. A preformatted search of the patent landscape also enhances the technology description and matching service. In an attempt to increase switching costs, TechEx is providing links to the information systems of strategic partners, including aggregating services that target the life sciences market. This makes it difficult for corporations to use a competing exchange, since their "supplier" is tied directly to TechEx.

REVENUE MODEL

TechEx offers completely free access to research institutions to encourage technology listings. An annual fee charged for corporate membership allows unlimited use of the system by the organization (rather than per user license). As TechEx develops value enhancements and is able to become instrumental to the technology transfer process, the company plans to charge a transaction fee for deals closed through the system. Anticipating demand for industry data generated by the trading system, TechEx plans to publish technology trends and charge users fees for access to this information.

CONFIDENTIALITY AND NEUTRALITY

TechEx users are aware of technology sources but not of who else is looking at the technology. The system indicates how many other companies are looking at the same technology. Member profiles are maintained in absolute confidentiality so that neither competing corporations nor researchers are privy to others' interests.

For further information
Intellectual Property Technology Exchange, Inc.
25 Science Park, Box 20
New Haven, CT 06511
1-203-865-5522
jerry.williamson@techex.com

Bibliography

Journals and magazines we took information from include *Business 2.0, Business Week, Forbes, Industry Standard, Inter@ctive Week, Red Herring, The Economist,* and *WIRED.*

Andersen Consulting. *eEurope Takes Off,* 1999. www.ac.com/showcase/ecommerce/ecom_efuture.html.

Andersen Consulting. *Your Choice,* 1998. www.ac.com/showcase/ecommerce/ecom_efuture.html.

Arthur Andersen. Independent report on MetalSite's business practices. metalsite.net/Welcome_to_MetalSite.cfm?target=admin/businessprinciples.cfm&ads=ad_bizprince.cfm.

Blankenhorn, Dana. "B2B Revolution." IntellectualCapital.com, 3 June 1999.

Bloomberg, Michael. *Bloomberg by Bloomberg.* New York: Wiley, 1997.

A Blueprint for Success, Toronto Stock Exchange, 8 October 1998.

Booz Allen & Hamilton and the Economist Intelligence Unit. *Competing in the Digital Age: How the Internet Will Transform Business,* 1999. Summary available at www.bah.com.

"BrokerTec," *Euromoney*, September 1999.

"B2B Boom: The Web's Trillion Dollar Secret," *Business 2.0*, September 1999.

Cairncross, Frances. *The Death of Distance*. London: Orion Business Books, 1997.

"Catex Obtains Capital and Commitments for Future Trading" (Catex press release). info.Catex.com/hamilton/Catex/press? articleID=11.

"Catex Reinsurance Reports 100th Deal: Electronic Transaction System Broadens Types of Postings," *Journal of Commerce*, 17 February 1999. info.Catex.com/hamilton/Catex/newsArticle?article ID=17.

Chicago Board of Trade. www.cbot.com/pointsofinterest/visitor/about_backgrounder.html.

Derivatives Supplement, *Financial Times*, 20 September 1999.

"dyb.com," *The Economist*, 18 September 1999.

Elamin, Ahmed. "Tech Tattle," *Royal Gazette* (Bermuda), October 1999.

Fell, Robert, Susan Selwyn, and W. William A. Woods. *The Right Way Forward. A Review of the Stock Exchange of Hong Kong's Monopoly Status*, International Securities Consultancy Research Report. Hamilton, Bermuda: ISI Publications, 1994.

Gartner Group. *Triggering the B2B Electronic Commerce Explosion*, 26 January 2000. www.gartnergroup.com/public/static/aboutgg/pressrel/pr012600c.html.

Gates, Bill. *Business @ The Speed of Thought: Using a Digital Nervous System*. New York: Warner Books, 1999.

The Global Market Forecast for Internet Usage and Commerce: Based on Internet Commerce Market Model (Version 5). CITY: International Data Corp., 1999.

Goldman Sachs. *B2B: 2B or not 2B?* Goldman Sachs Investment Research on E-Commerce/Internet, 14 September 1999.

Goldman Sachs. *Goldman Sachs Investment Research on Internet Technology,* 9 November 1998.

Hagel, John III, and Arthur G. Armstrong. *Net Gain: Expanding Markets through Virtual Communities.* Cambridge, MA: Harvard Business School Press, 1997.

Hagel, John III, and Marc Singer. *Net Worth: Shaping Markets When Customers Make the Rules.* Cambridge, MA: Harvard Business School Press, 1999.

"The Heyday of Auctions," *The Economist,* 23–30 July 1999.

IOSCO. Core Principles for Securities Market Regulations.

Kelly, Kevin. *New Rules for the New Economy: 10 Radical Strategies for a Connected World.* New York: Viking, 1998.

Lappin, Todd. "Get Rich . . . Quixtar!" *Business 2.0,* August 1999.

Lief, Varda. *Anatomy of New Market Models.* Cambridge, MA: Forrester Research, Inc., 1999.

Martin, James. *After the Internet: Alien Intelligence.* Washington, DC: Capital Press, 2000.

Martin, James. *Cypercorp: The New Business Revolution.* New York: Amacom, 1996.

Moore, Geoffrey A. *Crossing the Chasm: Marketing and Selling High-Tech Products to Mainstream Customers.* New York: HarperBusiness, 1995.

Moore, Geoffrey A. *Inside the Tornado.* New York: HarperBusiness, 1995.

Mougayar, Walid. *Opening Digital Markets: Battle Plans and Business Strategies for Internet Commerce.* New York: McGraw Hill, 1998.

Offshore News Online. www.offshoreon.com.

On-line. Offshore (Bermuda Stock Exchange corporate brochure). www.bsx.com.

Resizing On-line Business Trade. Cambridge, MA: Forrester Research, Inc., 1998.

Sawhney, Mahanbir, and Steven Kaplan. "Let's Get Vertical," *Business 2.0*, September 1999.

"A Virtual Trading Option for the Reinsurance Arena," *Insurance Networking*, 1 May 1999. info.Catex.com/hamilton/Catex/news Article?articleID=18.

Warner, Bernhard, and Miguel Helft. "How Culture Clash Sank the Toys "R" Us Deal," *Industry Standard*, 30 August/6 September 1999.

Warner, Fara. "General Motors Looks to the Future with Internet Unit," *Wall Street Journal*, 11 August 1999.

INDEX